Matthew Pinkowski's Special Summer

written and illustrated by

Patrick Quinn

Eagle Creek Publications
Prior Lake, Minnesota

Library of Congress Cataloging-in-Publication Data
Quinn, Patrick, 1950-
    Matthew Pinkowski's Special Summer / written and
illustrated by Patrick Quinn.
        p.   cm.
    Summary: Personal challenges such as learning
disabilities and deafness do not prevent thirteen-year-old
Matthew and his friends from having a summer filled
with adventure.
    ISBN 0-930323-82-3
    [1. Deaf—Fiction. 2. Learning disabilities—
Fiction. 3. Physically handicapped—Fiction. 4. Friend-
ship—Fiction.]
I. title
PZ7.Q4195Mat 1991
[Fic]—dc20   91-10982
                                                      CIP
                                                       AC

Cover illustration by Laura Stutzman.

Eagle Creek Publications
14160 Rolling Oaks Circle N.E.
Prior Lake, Minnesota 55372

**To my parents, Joseph and Irene Quinn,
who nurtured my earliest creative efforts.**

I would like to thank the following people who helped me in writing this book: my loving wife Mary, for her constant encouragement; Margaret Wangensteen, my writing mentor and friend; Margaret Sticha, for her expert word processing; Robyn Twito, my editor at Gallaudet University Press, who saw promise in Matthew's story and guided it to its present form; and my past and present students, who continue to teach me as much as I teach them.

Chapter 1

Adventure. That's the word that describes the most wonderful summer imaginable and the word that almost got my new friends and me into some big danger. My name is Matthew, Matthew Pinkowski, and I'm thirteen. My friends Sandy, Tommy, and Laura spent the summer with me and I would like to share the story of that special summer and what I found out about me.

Adventure is a word that my sixth-grade teacher last year, Mr. Wetzel, used a lot. "Adventure," Mr. Wetzel would say, "there's no adventure any more. People used to live with danger and excitement every day of their lives. There were roving mountain lions and marauding bears. People used to hunt wild animals for food."

He would walk quietly down the aisle as if he were stalking something. He snuck up on Jeffrey Drobnick who was sleeping with his head on the desk. "There weren't any supermarkets in those days," he said, tapping Jeffrey on the back of the head. "Tribes of primitive people had to be ready to attack other tribes and be ready to be attacked, too. It was simply the way people lived for millions of years."

Mr. Wetzel looked out the window toward some faraway place. Then he turned his head back toward us. "Suddenly," he said, "because man is so smart, or maybe because he is not so smart, he's taken all the adventure out of life. He's safe. He sleeps behind strong walls. All the dangerous animals are in zoos or live far up in northern Minnesota, in Canada, or in Alaska."

Mr. Wetzel got excited when he talked about these things. He excited some of us kids, too. It would be great, I thought, to live in the wilds and hunt and build leaf shelters, to sneak silently through the forests having an adventure every hour or so. I knew I could do it, and I wouldn't have to read or write, either.

I broke my news to Mom on the last day of school, while I was helping her with the dishes. I told her straight out that when I turned sixteen, I would be moving up to the north woods where I would live off the land. Mom wasn't too thrilled. She doesn't always take me seriously, but she hardly ever ignores me. "What do you plan to do for food? You need your eight essential amino acids you know." She didn't look up from the dishes.

"Bear meat," was my answer. "The North is full of bears."

"What about clothes? You know if you leave you'll have to go with the clothes you came in."

"What do you mean?" I asked.

"No clothes. You came in no clothes," was her reply.

"That's no problem. Bear skins. That's what the Indians used."

"Have you ever heard what the mosquitoes, the deer flies, and the wood ticks are like in northern Minnesota during the summer, dear?" She held up one of the wine glasses to check for water spots.

"Bear grease, Mom," I answered, casually holding up another wine glass to the light. "That keeps 'em away."

"Yuk!" she said wrinkling her nose.

"Sure," I responded, rubbing off a little water spot. "The Ojibwe Indians used to rub bear grease all over themselves to keep off the bugs."

"It doesn't sound like it would do much for the romance in their lives," Mom commented.

"I don't know much about that, Mom. Romance isn't of much interest to us wilderness men. We go it alone."

"Well, be sure to write," she said, and turned on the garbage disposal.

I had a little better luck in talking to Dad about my plan. He set the paper down. "It might be a good idea to sleep in the backyard for a while to get the 'feel' of the wild. You could study up on the wilderness during the day. When you get the hang of it, then you could try camping in the woods. You could kind of ease into it."

That plan sounded pretty good to me, so I pitched my little orange pup tent under the dead elm tree in the backyard.

I slept with the screen flap wide open in case any wild animals came along. You're likely to miss adventures with the screen flap zipped. The only wild animals that came by that night were the neighbor's gray tabby cat and six thousand starving mosquitoes. The three thousand inside the tent called to the three thousand outside the tent. I think the ones inside were trying to help the ones outside find the flap. I zipped the flap shut and started slapping my hands together. After about half an hour I had gotten two thousand, nine hundred, and ninety-nine of them. That last mosquito was one of the things that kept me up most of the first night.

The other thing that kept me awake the first night was the back door light. Mom switched it on after she thought I had gone to sleep. Adventures don't happen with back door lights on. So I crawled out, unscrewed the bulb, and closed the back door, which she had left open for me.

I really didn't have what you'd call an adventure that night, but I did enjoy the sky. It was lit by a half-moon that looked like a cereal bowl turned on its side. Stars really do twinkle. I started to count the stars three times. Some of the tinier ones disappeared if I looked at them for more than a couple seconds.

Late that night the wind picked up and the mosquitoes went away. The big elm tree had enough leaves left on it to catch quite a bit of wind. The wood from the elm made strange, low, creaking noises that sounded like groans. I remembered that the tree was dying. Then the noises sounded like very sad voices coming from inside the trunk. The wind puffed and snapped at the sides of the tent.

I think I slept for an hour or two before every bird in Minnesota started singing, chirping, whistling, and warbling in our backyard. A couple days later we moved.

Chapter 2

Stillwater, Minnesota. That's the town I moved to last June. Believe me, it wasn't my idea to move. Dad got a raise, and he and Mom decided they didn't like living in the big city anymore. Our new town is close enough for Dad to drive to work, but too far for me to bike to visit my old friends.

I wasn't happy about it, at first. It's not that I was angry or afraid. It was more of a helpless feeling, like when we had our old dog Lucas put to sleep. But there wasn't much I could do about it. At least Mom and Dad listened to why I didn't want to move. We moved anyway.

Stillwater. Well, there's lots of water here all right. The St. Croix River runs right past the city. And the city stretches from the river's edge clear to the top of the tree-covered bluff. Across the valley is another bluff just like it, only there's no town on it. That's the Wisconsin side. We live on the Minnesota side, at the very top of the bluff. From our backyard I can see all the way to Wisconsin.

The water is never still that I've ever been able to tell. There are always waves—little ones from swimmers or raindrops; middle-sized ones from breezes and small boats; and big, white-capped ones from the huge cabin cruisers that wander up and down the river. Weekends are especially wavy because all these things are likely to happen at the same time.

The sign as you drive into town says Stillwater, Minnesota, Birthplace of Minnesota. The sign always sounds to me like all the Minnesota babies are born right here. I found out later from an older woman named Mert that the state's government got its start here more than a hundred years ago.

The whole valley back then, she told me, from here to clear up past Taylor's Falls, was covered with huge pine trees. Along the river bluffs and as far back as they could get, loggers cut down every pine tree in sight. They dragged them down to the St. Croix River and floated them down to Stillwater. So Stillwater used to be a wild logging town. Some people got rich, some people went broke, most people worked really hard, and a few people even got killed. Stillwater's still here, but all the pine trees are gone. Now the bluffs behind our house are covered with other kinds of trees — ones whose leaves have to be raked in the fall.

When I first moved here I decided that the "still" in Stillwater had to do with the people. People sat still on their decks and cooked in those black grills with the round covers. Some sat still on the boat landing and stared at their fishing bobbers going up and down, up and down, all afternoon. Even downtown, where people actually moved, they moved so slowly it seemed like they were standing still.

In St. Paul, at least there was some action—ball games, buses, fire engines, jets overhead, the lady next door screaming. It was all great as far as I was concerned. Mom didn't think it was so great. Dad didn't think it was so great, either. Nobody asked me. So here we are in Stillwater.

I wrote all about Stillwater in a letter to my old friend, Robert, in St. Paul. I spent a whole morning writing that stupid letter. When I was addressing the envelope Mom told me it wasn't long distance to call St. Paul on the telephone. Stillwater is only fifteen miles from St. Paul. It seemed like such a long way. I sent off the letter anyway since I had spent so much time on it.

Right off, I should say that reading and writing aren't easy for me. I can plow through most reading if the words aren't too long, but it takes me about five times as long as most other kids. I read words so slowly that I usually can't remember what I just read. My special education teacher, Ms. Schmidke, told me that a little part of my brain doesn't work exactly like most people's. It's hard for me to make out the letters fast enough because so many of them look so much alike. It embarrasses me a lot of the time. Ms. Schmidke told me that I'm plenty smart. I didn't really believe her, though, until the end of the summer I'm telling you about.

Chapter 3

My dad is a do-it-yourselfer. I admire him for that. He changes the oil in our car. I get the tools and pour the dirty, slimy oil into a big container. He fixes leaky faucets. I get the bucket and mop. He builds decks and closet shelves. I get the tools he forgets. I think Dad is more of a do-it-ourselfer.

One of Dad's do-it-ourself projects is ordering wood for the fireplace. I stack it. A little while after we moved in Dad ordered a big load of wood. We had resealed the blacktop driveway the evening before, so the truck couldn't drive to the backyard. The load had to be dumped at the end of the driveway, practically in the street.

Before I tell about what happened, I have to tell about our street, Valley View Drive. Mom and Dad think it's a poetic name. I liked our old street name in St. Paul—Wilson. Wilson was a straight street. There were cross streets at the end of the block. You knew how far it was from one place to another by counting the blocks. You could give directions people could follow.

Valley View Drive is another story. It begins at the top of the bluff and winds back and forth along the wooded hill, making two sharp curves before it gets to our place. The road is steep, dropping to the right as you look out from our house. Then a little ways past our house it really gets steep. I always walk my bike down that hill. A neighbor told my dad that the hill is so steep he can expect to pay for a new brake job every two years. It's a good thing Dad and I also do brake jobs.

When stacking firewood, it helps if you think you're stronger than you really are. That day I imagined I was the Incredible Hulk. I rolled my jeans up

to my knees, took off my shirt, mussed up my hair, and hunched over like a big gorilla. Then I picked up the logs and stacked them in the wheelbarrow.

After growling and hauling logs, my voice was hoarse and my muscles were tired. I had just loaded the wheelbarrow for the fifth time. It was time for the Hulk to take five. I lay down in the shade and stared up at the sky. The clouds were gray and white, gray in the middle and bright white on the edges.

I was doing all this cloud watching so I almost didn't hear the scream the first time. When I heard the second scream, I jumped up so fast I fell right down again.

The screams had come from a short-haired blond girl who was sprinting down the street alongside a moving station wagon. That girl must really want to go along, I thought, the way she keeps racing alongside the car and screaming. She kept grabbing at a door handle, but it wouldn't open. The station wagon was picking up speed and her actions were starting to look dangerous and crazy. I figured most parents would at least stop and let her have it about being a spoiled brat.

The station wagon was about a house away from our place. I wanted to get a good look at this driver who seemed not to care that the girl was likely to get hurt. But there was no driver. Just a boy sitting on the passenger side. He looked as scared as the girl. Then I realized that the engine wasn't running and the car was going faster.

The screaming girl suddenly lost her footing on the loose sand. She tucked and did two terrific somersaults. Somehow, she got back to her feet, but the car had slipped away from her. The car was almost at our house. The girl screamed "Tommy!" as she continued her crazy run. About this time, I got my mouth shut. I don't remember thinking about it, though. Before you could say Incredible Hulk, I dumped the loaded wheelbarrow into the street, just before the station wagon zoomed by. The car bumped and clunked over the logs, hopped the curb, and smacked into our maple tree.

Chapter 4

Stillwater never quite seemed still again after the station wagon skidded to a stop in my front yard. It was a special summer vacation being delivered right to my door.

The first thing I remember after the car hit the tree was the blond-haired girl screaming at the boy inside. The scream sounded like it was half scare, half anger, and half relief. I know that adds up to more than one scream, but it was quite a scream. The girl ran up to the car door and pulled the handle. When it didn't open, she made two fists and shouted, "Unlock the door, Tommy, before I rip it off and come in after you!"

Tommy quickly pulled up on the lock button. The girl yanked the door open before Tommy had time to let go of it. This caused him to flip head first, right onto the grass. His glasses fell off, broken.

By now, several neighbors had dashed out. One-half of them was telling the other half what happened. A couple of women tended to Tommy's broken glasses and the blond-haired girl's bloody knees. Some of the neighbors called the blond-haired girl Sandy.

Sandy pointed to me several times and told them what I had done. We hadn't met most of the neighbors yet, so I figured that was the reason no one had said anything to me.

Then Sandy walked over with a serious look on her face. She paused, lifted her eyebrows a little, and said, "Do you talk?"

I remembered I was still in my Hulk outfit with the mussed hair, rolled-up jeans, and no shirt. To make things worse, there were grass clippings stuck to my back from when I had been lying on the freshly cut yard.

"Ah . . . yes, I talk." I reached down to unroll my jeans. "In fact, I talk just fine."

"That's good," Sandy said, grinning. "I think you saved my brother's life. I don't know what would have happened if he'd gone down that hill. What you did was the smartest and fastest thinking I've ever seen." She lowered her eyebrows. "What's your name, anyway?"

"Matthew. What's yours?"

"Sandy. Sandy Larson. What's your last name?"

"Pinkowski," I answered.

"Pinkowski? That's a different name. I'll bet you get a lot of nicknames."

I nodded. "Kids used to call me Pincushion instead of Pinkowski. They thought it was pretty funny. It's Polish." Sandy looks really hard at you while she listens. I couldn't think of anything to say for a few seconds. "Hey," I said, finally thinking of something, "that was some tuck and double roll you did back there. You even landed on your feet."

Sandy smiled with her eyes. They're a pale, pale almost-gray blue. "Thanks, but I really didn't even know I did it. I've done that so many times in gymnastics I probably did it automatically."

"Well, automatic or not, it was good," I added.

"Thanks again, but you're the one who saved Tommy." Before I could say anything more the rest of the neighbors came over to talk to me.

"Young man, that was a brave thing you did," said an older woman with big blue glasses and a tiny red mouth.

"That was quick thinking if I've ever seen it," a tall, thin woman remarked nodding her head.

"Amazing," another person added.

"Unbelievable," said a heavyset man with grass-stained shoes and a rake.

Everyone was more excited than I was. Things had happened so fast that it didn't seem possible that all that praise was for me.

Sandy and Tommy's mom had just been told by a neighbor what had happened. Before the neighbor could finish the whole story, Mrs. Larson dashed out the front door and raced down the street in her stocking feet.

Mrs. Larson was so upset it took a couple of neighbors to calm her down. They kept reminding her that Tommy and Sandy were just fine and that cars can always be repaired. With all the attention on Mrs. Larson for a minute, I had a chance to brush the grass off my back and put on my shirt. When someone told Mrs. Larson that I had been the one to knock the logs in front of the car, she ran right over and hugged me so hard I almost stopped breathing. If the hug didn't kill me I thought the embarrassment would.

From over Mrs. Larson's shoulder I suddenly saw my mom on the sidewalk staring in disbelief. I waved. "Hi, Mom. This is Mrs. Larson."

Mrs. Larson finally let go of me and turned toward Mom. "Are you this young man's mother?"

Before Mom could answer, Mrs. Larson started hugging her, too. "Your wonderful son saved my son's life. What a wonderful boy!"

Mom caught her breath. "Yes, we think he's pretty wonderful, too. We're very proud of him."

Meanwhile, Sandy had walked back to help Tommy find a lens that had popped out of his glasses. If it was anything like the other lens, it was as thick as the bottom of a pop bottle. Tommy has a pretty normal-looking face except for glasses so thick they make his eyes look like they're sunk an inch inside his head. Anyway, Sandy was hunched over frowning at the ground. Her knees were still bleeding, but she didn't seem to notice.

"Sandy," her mother called, "let's get home and tend to those knees of yours. Don't worry about the lens. It'll turn up. Tommy has another pair of glasses at home, anyway. Come on. Tommy, you help clean up the logs, then you come, too. We're going to have a little talk."

Tommy and a bunch of the neighbors helped me pick up the logs. Before long, the police came to check things out. Then a tow truck dragged the station wagon someplace. After that the man from the town's newspaper, *The Stillwater Times*, arrived. I didn't know what a human interest story was until some people from the TV station in Minneapolis came to our house. They did a short story about all the things that happened, which wasn't much, although anybody who watched it on TV would have thought different. I watched it at six o'clock and again at ten o'clock. I thought my nose looked kind of big and I said "ah" about twenty times. Besides that, I looked and sounded okay.

It was a big day. I don't remember sleeping much that night.

Chapter 5

The next morning I found Sandy and Tommy weeding their backyard vegetable garden. There were lots of rows of green plants whose names I didn't know. Mom didn't have a vegetable garden. She'd been born and raised on a farm and had more than her share of gardening. She swore that the next time she got that close to the soil would be when she was buried in it. I didn't think that was very funny and I told her so.

Tommy saw me coming across the lawn and said "Hi." All that summer I never saw him grouchy or mad. Tommy is one of the friendliest kids I know. You don't even have to be nice to him first. In fact, you can even be mean to him and he's still nice. Sandy told me kids at school are mean to him sometimes, but it doesn't seem to bother him.

Sandy looked up and said, "Hey Matthew, I saw you on the TV news last night. Boy was that exciting! You're famous!"

"Yeah, I know," I answered in an embarrassed way. "My dad videotaped it and everything. All the relatives are gonna see it for the next fifty or sixty years at every Christmas party, birthday, and family reunion." I put my hands in my pockets. "It's really exciting, but I think people are making too big a deal of it."

"No, they aren't!" said a voice from behind me. I recognized Mrs. Larson, Sandy and Tommy's mom, the woman who did all the hugging the day before. "What you did deserves all the attention it can get! Few people in their entire lives get the chance to save another's life. You had a chance and look at what you did. I've called the mayor and the Stillwater Chamber of Commerce to see if they can find some small way of recognizing what you've done."

"Mrs. Larson, you shouldn't have!" I said, and I meant it.

"Nonsense!" she replied. "You saved a life. Selfless things like that should not go unrecognized." She lowered her eyebrows, just the way Sandy did. "People only seem to get attention these days for holding up a bank or killing somebody. We need some heroes to offset all the creeps."

"Well, what do you think they would want to do about it—the mayor and the Chamber of Commerce?" I asked.

"I'm not really sure they'll do anything," Mrs. Larson answered. "I imagine the city is getting all geared up for Pioneer Days. They might not even have time to consider my call. Maybe you don't have to worry, Matthew."

"Don't be too sure, Ma," said Sandy, grinning. "Remember last year? That guy who saw the UFO over the river? He was the only one who saw it." Sandy bent over and with both hands pulled out several radishes. "That's the same guy who keeps bumping his head on stop signs when he's walking downtown. The newspaper covered his UFO story and the next thing you know he's on a float in the Pioneer Days parade, compliments of the Stillwater Chamber of Commerce. The guy's a hero."

"A float?" I swallowed hard.

"You bet," Sandy said, nodding.

Mrs. Larson cradled freshly picked carrots, tomatoes, and radishes in her arm and headed to the house. Tommy followed close behind.

I noticed that Tommy had a peculiar way of walking. He leaned forward some and held his hands a little in front of him, as if he were always ready to stop himself from falling. As he walked alongside the house toward the back door, he slid one hand along the wall, the way a little kid does who is still learning to walk.

"Sandy, you and Tommy don't seem like you're from the same family. It's really none of my business or anything, but I was wondering about it."

"That's okay." Sandy watched Tommy disappear into the house. "Tommy's my adopted brother. He's a year older than me. Mom and Dad adopted Tommy when he was two months old. A couple of months later Mom got pregnant with me. We're in the same grade, but we don't have many classes together. Tommy gets lots of special help at school. Learning doesn't come easily to him."

"Yeah, I knew some kids at my old school who got special help. They were in regular classes part of the time and then they'd go out every once in a while to a special classroom."

"Yeah," Sandy continued, "that's the same thing. Tommy isn't too coordinated, but he's a whole lot better than he used to be. He pretty much ran around the house wrecking stuff for the first few years. Finally, Mom and Dad got some medicine from the doctor that helped slow him down. He was so hyper that Mom and Dad almost went crazy. She told me last year that they almost got a divorce because they were so grouchy and tired all the time. I guess they didn't have time to be nice to each other."

Sandy knelt down and pulled off some dandelion tops. "I used to hate it. With Mom and Dad fighting and pulling Tommy off the drapes, they barely had any time left for me. Sometimes I felt like I hated him. I wanted to flush Tommy down the toilet. I pretty much had to fend for myself. But that's okay, because now I know I can take care of myself."

I didn't know what to say, so I didn't say anything.

Sandy thought for a moment. "He's doing better in school lately, but he still has a long way to go. Tommy has trouble with reading, writing, spelling, handwriting, and even talking."

"What do you mean, 'talking'?" I asked.

"It mainly has to do with questions. He asks questions as long as there is a live body in front of him to answer."

"I didn't notice."

"Give him a little time. His questions are usually pretty good ones, so watch out. He knows the answers to most of them, too. He mainly asks questions because he likes asking." Sandy twisted the yellow dandelion between her thumb and forefinger. "There's a big plus for Tommy, though. He has an unbelievable memory for . . . well . . . I'm not sure how to put it. Let's just say he's something like a walking *Guiness Book of World Records*." She started to count on her fingers. "He remembers telephone numbers he hears on TV commercials, batting averages of baseball players I've never heard of, windchill index charts, the accumulated snowfall on Lake Superior in 1978. . . Are you getting the idea, Matthew?" she said, squinting up at me. "He isn't too smart in some ways, but he really can remember some weird stuff."

I'd known kids like Tommy at my old school in St. Paul, except I don't think they had memories like Tommy's. To be really honest, I steered clear of those kids. With me being in special ed and them being in special ed, I sure didn't want anybody thinking I was like them.

I was in a different program for kids who were pretty smart but had trouble with reading or math. The kids like Tommy weren't too good at learning anything having to do with schoolwork. Sometimes, kids would make cracks about me being a slow learner because I had to go to a special room. It really burned me up, and if I hadn't been in school, there were a few times when I would have started slugging. Anyway, now I knew there was a slow learner living in my new neighborhood, and we were going to be in the same grade at the same school. It was depressing.

I asked Sandy, "What's it like being Tommy's sister? Does it make you feel kind of, well, embarrassed?"

"Sometimes," she replied, as she picked up a big pile of weeds and hauled them over to another, bigger pile of weeds by the edge of the garden. "You see, Tommy's so famous at school that kids still call me 'Tommy's sister.' I don't like that, but what I used to hate the most was having to watch him so much." Sandy squinted into the quickly rising morning sun as she looked at me, "I'll tell you more if you'll weed the broccoli, Matthew."

"Oh, sure. Which one is the broccoli? No, let me guess. Here it is. This must be the broccoli."

"Matthew," Sandy said, shaking her head, "you haven't gardened much, have you? These are weeds. These big green things you're standing on are the broccoli plants. Pull the weeds out and leave the broccoli. It's pretty easy."

I knelt down and started ripping weeds out. "Tell me more about you and Tommy."

"Okay, like the bus, I had to make sure he got on the right one after school. I had to sit next to him most of the time, too. I even got into a couple of fights when some boys started making fun of him."

"I guess you held your own," I said, trying to be funny.

Sandy shrugged her shoulders, "I did all right, but I don't like fighting."

"Fighting hurts more than it looks like it should, doesn't it?" I asked her, as I joined my pile of weeds with the bigger one. "One time I tried to karate chop a kid and my knuckles swelled up for a week."

"Well, I don't know much about karate." Sandy continued, "I didn't have too many friends in the beginning because I spent so much time taking care of Tommy. Some kids avoided me. I think it was because my brother was with me so much. They thought if they were seen with us, other kids might think they weren't so smart, either. I don't know. Sometimes I felt like I just plain hated him, but that wasn't true. What I hated was being his sister all the time. Now he takes a lot better care of himself than he used to. I don't have to watch him so much. But yesterday was sure another story, that is, with him and the car."

Sandy looked down at the brown mud caked on her sneakers. She scraped some of the stubborn stuff off with her foot. "Know what? I learned something yesterday when that car was rolling down the hill. I had almost no idea how much I really care about my brother. I thought he was a pesky kid who sat across the table from me at supper and spilled milk every night. I thought about that a lot last night. I really think we're tied to brothers and moms and dads with hundreds and hundreds of ropes, all tied with tight knots. When he headed down that hill, it was like those knots and ropes were being pulled apart. I guess

I never knew the knots were there." Sandy looked at me straight on, which made me feel a little uneasy. I understood what she was saying.

"Yeah," I said, "my dog Lucas died last year. Sometimes, I forgot to feed him and brush him. I didn't ever think he'd be gone. It took a long time to get over that. I mean, him dying and all."

I helped Sandy weed for a while longer and we talked about kids we knew, teachers, basketball, scars, stitches, and athletic shoes. I also thought over the things she had said about her and Tommy. I felt pretty good she had told me all that. And I was glad to learn what a broccoli plant looked like.

Chapter 6

The phone rang the next morning about eight o'clock. Mom answered it. "Yes, I'm Matthew Pinkowski's mother. . . . Uh-huh. Yes, we are very proud of him. . . . Yes, it is rather remarkable. . . . Pioneer Days? Why yes, I've heard of it. It's in two weeks, isn't it?" Mom stopped talking except for an "uh-huh" every ten seconds or so. She kept smiling and glancing at me. I started to expect the worst. I got it.

"Oh, certainly! I'm sure he'd be honored." She was looking directly at me. "Should he wear anything special? . . . No, I don't think he has any buckskin clothes, but we may be able to find something. . . . A sign would be fine. . . . It's spelled P-I-N-K-O-W-S-K-I. . . . Yes, I hope it will fit on the sign, too. What time should he be there? . . . Thank-you. . . . Uh-huh. . . . Bye now."

"I have to clean my room that day, Mom. You know how I neglect my room. It'll probably take me from—what time did he say the parade started, ten o'clock? It'll take me from ten o'clock until whenever the parade gets over. I'm sure of it. Sorry, Mom. Duty calls and I cannot fail. That's just the kind of son I am. That's the way you brought me up. You and Dad have no one to blame but yourselves."

"I told them you'd be there, dear."

"But, Mom, I'll look so weird up there all by myself."

"You won't be all by yourself, Matthew. Miss Stillwater will be sitting next to you. She'll be dressed like an Indian princess. Boy scouts will be all around the float dressed like Indian braves. I hear they have life-sized manikins of deer, raccoons, and even a fifty-year-old black bear named Snuffy. He was stuffed in a standing position and he'll be at the front of the float. You, Matthew, are the guest of honor and will be on the highest part of the float with Miss Stillwater."

I stuck my fingers down my throat, pretending to gag. Mom ignored me. "But Mom, what does dumping logs in the street have to do with parades?"

"The Chamber of Commerce believes you are the person in the community who, during the last year, has best shown the pioneer quality of unselfish bravery."

I thought about how hard Sandy had tried to stop the car and she'd even been hurt. "Mom, do you know who's really brave?"

"Yes, dear, you are. After all, you saved a life. I don't understand why this is bothering you so much. I would think you'd be delighted and excited and . . . proud. There's nothing wrong with feeling proud, just as long as you don't get too big-headed about it."

"Okay, Mom." That was that. I was in the parade. Mom was busy running water for the dishes. After a few seconds a thought came to me. "Say, Mom, do girls ever win this award?"

"No reason they can't win it. Women can be just as brave as men. Why do you ask?"

I shrugged, "Oh, I was just wondering."

We were leaving the next day for a week's vacation at my grandparents. I decided to have a good long think before we left. I wasn't really sure why, but being honored in this parade felt wrong. I knew that I did think quickly, but it didn't seem especially brave. For sure, it was not the kind of brave that Mr. Wetzel talked about. I hadn't come close to getting hurt or anything. Sandy was the brave one. I might be brave, too, but I hadn't yet had a real chance to find out.

After a bit more thinking, I came up with a plan that made sense to me. It would take care of the problem about who was the brave one and get rid of the bad feeling I had about the parade.

Just before we left on vacation I went over to Sandy's and asked her if she would come with Mom and Dad and me to the parade. She said she would. Now I knew I could make my plan work.

Chapter 7

I spent the next week at my grandparent's house in Lake City. Lake City is in Minnesota and, like Stillwater, it's on a river. It's on the Mississippi River. In fact, the water going down the St. Croix River past Stillwater flows right down into the Mississippi at a town called Hastings. After that, the two rivers travel on together and go right past Lake City. I wondered if I spit in the river at Stillwater when we left, would I get to Lake City before my spit did? I decided that I'd get there first because once Dad starts the car he doesn't stop until he gets where he's going.

I can only remember Dad ever stopping twice. Once, so I could throw up. He left the car running, though. The other time he stopped was at a root beer stand. Actually, he stopped for directions and decided he'd better buy something. He left the car running that time, too. We made it to Lake City in record time—one hour and fourteen minutes.

After we visited in the living room for a while, Mom told them all about the parade and that I needed a buckskin outfit. Grandma Mary said she still had Dad's old Davy Crockett coonskin hat and pants with fringe and everything. And she knew right where to look. The attic was very neat. All the junk was sitting in perfect rows. The boxes were marked with magic markers telling what was inside. You would expect that there would be a lot of dust, but there wasn't. She kept her attic as clean as the rest of her house.

A single, dim light bulb hung in the center of the attic and made square, straight shadows on the rows of boxes. The sharp smell of mothballs was everywhere.

"Are you sure it's still here, Grandma?" I asked.

"It should be right about here." Grandma pulled down a small box from a shelf above the tiny attic window. It was marked Martin's Davy Crockett Paraphernalia. Grandma explained that paraphernalia means "stuff." She liked the sound of the word. She said it had style. Besides a big, tidy attic, Grandma also had a big vocabulary.

The Davy Crockett outfit fit pretty good, except for the hat, which was too small, and the shirt, which wasn't even there. The pants fit fine. Grandpa suggested that Dad and I see Uncle Buck. He could fix us up with a shirt.

After lunch, Dad and I drove on some old boondockey, gravel back roads to find Cletus "Buck" McNellen. He's a distant uncle or cousin or something of Dad's.

"Uncle Buck," Dad said, "is the best deer hunter in Wabasha County, if not the best in southeastern Minnesota. He makes the finest deerskin clothes around, and he wears them everyplace his wife will let him."

"Like where, Dad?"

"He'd wear them to church, but she won't have any part of it," Dad answered. "People all the way in the Twin Cities drive out to have Buck make clothes for them. He cleans, stretches, dries, and tans the deer hides. He can cut a perfect pattern just by looking at a person."

We drove down a long, dusty driveway toward a tidy farmhouse surrounded by a few odd-shaped buildings and a faded barn. Uncle Buck, I found out, is a retired farmer who rents out his land to a neighbor. I didn't recognize any of the plants growing along the driveway. I was sure they weren't raising broccoli. At least, none I could see.

I don't think I've ever ridden up to a farm where some big dog didn't growl and bark and lunge at the car. Dad and I always wait in the car until the owners come out and scold the dog. Of course, the owners always say the dog doesn't bite. I never believe them. I'd bet a hundred dollars if I got out of a car when the owner wasn't around, I'd lose a pant leg just like that.

Mrs. Buck came out the side door. Three sleeping cats opened their eyes to check us out and then closed them again. She was a heavy woman, so she walked with a side-to-side motion. She wiped her hands on a big, white apron and didn't smile at first. She had bluish-gray hair and eyes to match. Wire-rim glasses sat low on her short nose and her jaw was lost in her cheeks. She called off the dogs, "You two, hush now." They barked once more and Mrs. Buck kicked at one of them, but missed. "Hush, I said."

Dad rolled down the window. "Hello, Aunt Lizzie, remember me?" She still didn't smile. "Martin," Dad continued. "Martin Pinkowski." Then she smiled, and her large cheeks lifted up, making her eyes disappear some.

"Oh," she laughed. "I didn't know you at first. Come on out of there. We've not seen you for a couple years now, right? Who's this with you? This your boy?"

"This is Matthew, Aunt Lizzie. He's grown quite a lot since the last time you saw him."

I waited for the one about how much I'd grown since the last time she'd seen me. I didn't have to wait long.

"The last time I seen you, Matthew, you were this big." She held her hand to her waist. "You look just like your daddy when he was your age. My, my, don't the time fly by." She smiled kindly, sighed, and shook her head slowly. "I reckon you'd like to see Buck." She shouted toward one of the sheds across the driveway. "Buck! Buck!" Aunt Lizzie looked at Dad and shook her head. "Buck, he don't hear so good lately. Too much gunfire by his ears, the doctor says." She shouted louder, but he still didn't come out. "Just a second, I'll fetch him."

She walked her side-to-side walk across the dusty driveway and up to the shed. Buck stepped out into the sunlight. He looked like someone from an old western movie. He was lean and a little bent over. The hair on his head was pure silver and his long, pointed beard was silver with streaks of black in it. His face was dark brown, and seemed even darker because of his silver-black beard. There were deep lines across his forehead and at the corners of his black eyes.

Uncle Buck wore a loose-fitting, pullover shirt and buckskin pants. Long fringe along the outside seams of the pants dangled and danced as he walked. His moccasins made no noise at all.

"Say there, it's been a long time," Dad said slowly and clearly so Uncle Buck could understand him. He shook Uncle Buck's hand.

"Yeah, been a stretch, hadn't it? Good ta see you, Martin. How's that pretty girl you married?"

"Just fine, Uncle Buck. She's been student teaching at a school in St. Paul. She's going to finish her degree this fall and start teaching as soon as a job opens up."

Uncle Buck stuck out his lower lip. "Is that so? Pretty, with brains, too. You're looking pretty good yerself, young fella. A little pale, maybe. Been out in God's sunlight at all since winter?"

"Oh, not too much yet," Dad said. "But it's the beginning of summer. Just give me a chance."

Uncle Buck looked at me. "Who's this little fella with you?"

"This is Matthew, Uncle Buck. He's been out here before, but it's been a while."

"He looks like you, all right. 'Specially around the eyes. But he's got a might more color than his daddy." He winked at me.

Uncle Buck and Dad sat on the porch and talked and drank iced tea. I drank some cold well water with lemon and sugar. Aunt Lizzie disappeared into the house. Uncle Buck and Dad talked about who'd married lately, who'd had babies, who was going into the priesthood or convent, who was laid up, and who had died. The "who had died" part was sad. Many of Uncle Buck and Aunt Lizzie's old friends, brothers, and sisters seemed to have died on them. The conversation slowed down and they got quiet. Dad and Uncle Buck stared at their hands or off at something far away. I wondered if they were remembering.

"Uncle Buck," Dad said after a lull, "we're hoping you can help us." Dad told him about my saving Tommy's life and the parade and our need for a buckskin shirt. Uncle Buck leaned forward on the porch swing and took a closer look at my face.

"That was mighty quick thinkin' there, Matthew. So everyone treatin' you like a hero now?"

"Yes, sir."

"Well, how do you feel about being a big hero?" he asked.

"Well, Uncle Buck, I don't feel like I did all that much. I mean, not that Tommy's life isn't important . . . but you see, I just dumped the logs over. That's all."

Uncle Buck surprised me. "I know 'xactly what you mean, Matthew. Somethin' like that happened to me once when I was deer huntin' over near Kellogg. That was years ago." He looked off across the yard like he was looking off across the years.

"It was in Cooke's Valley. I was out with my nephew Daniel. I'd just downed a good-sized buck near Kinnebec's stream. Now, I don't know how much you know about deer huntin', Matthew, but a good-sized buck can be a dangerous animal when he's trapped or hurt. That rack on the top of his head ain't just for mountin' over fireplaces. And we did a pretty dumb thing. We set our rifles against a tree and walked over to get a closer look. We were almost to the animal when it stumbled to its feet and lunged at Daniel, knockin' him plumb off his feet and into the stream. The buck was makin' to go after Daniel, again. Without thinkin', I went after the buck, grabbed him by the rack, and held on for dear life. Next thing you know, the buck and I tumbled into the stream. Good thing it was deeper than usual because of the melting snow. I held that big, kickin' animal under the water until he stopped kickin'."

Uncle Buck shook his head and smiled. "You know, Matthew, it happened so fast I didn't even have time to get scared. Daniel blew that story up so you'd of thought I fought off a whole gang of grizzly bears with my bare hands." Uncle Buck narrowed his eyes, "You know what I think brave is?" I shook my head. "It's when you got the scared feelin' in your stomach, in your arms, and in your legs. And part of you wants to freeze, and part of you wants to run and hide like a rabbit. If, with that feelin' a body does somethin' to help someone else, then that person's really brave."

"See Lizzie over there in the garden? She's braver than I am. She gave birth to six kids. Every time she knew it was gonna hurt like the dickens and she was scared. She never complained or talked about being scared, but I could tell. You live with somebody long enough, you can read their eyes. Matthew, why do you think women don't try to prove how tough they are, the way us men sometimes do?"

"I don't know, Uncle Buck. I guess I thought they weren't interested in that kind of thing."

"Well, they aren't. At least, most of them aren't. The way I see it, they know they're tough. That's why they don't run around findin' ways to prove it. In a way they're forced into it by nature. You know what, though, Matthew? It occurs to me, as I think back on all the fuss people have made about the things we did, neither of us really wanted or needed all the attention. I think . . . I think maybe that people need to give it. Maybe people need heroes. God knows there ain't many of 'em. Real heroes don't go lookin' to be heroes because then they'd be the selfish type and wouldn't be thinkin' about no one 'cept themselves. Heroes got to be ordinary people who are watchin' out for others. When the time comes—boom! They're ready!"

"I'll bet those Stillwater people need you on that float for their sake, not yours. You're just an ordinary kid who was ready. Who knows? Maybe, you'll inspire somebody else to be ready."

What Uncle Buck said made sense and has stuck with me since. I decided then that I was going to be on the float, and I would stop complaining about it. In fact, it became a duty.

Uncle Buck made a beautiful buckskin shirt with fringe on the front in the shape of a V. Long fringe hung down the side of each arm. Rawhide laced up the front to close the V-neck opening. He rummaged through a bunch of soft furs he kept in a heavy chest. He found a raccoon fur with a striped tail. Uncle Buck sewed it into a perfect hat with the tail hanging down the back.

Dad and I watched Uncle Buck work in his leather shed. As he worked he told us all about what he was doing. Uncle Buck explained that he had learned his craft as a young man from an old Indian named Two Rivers, who had lived many years ago on a reservation. On the walls of Uncle Buck's shed were color prints of fur traders and Indians on horseback and in canoes. The air in the room had a sharp smell of leather that I didn't get used to for almost an hour.

The time came when we had to be on our way. Dad lost the argument with Uncle Buck over whether or not we would pay him. He wouldn't take money. For a few seconds it even looked like they might get into a fight. But they laughed about it when they were done. I wore my new shirt and hat. Going down the driveway, I waved to Uncle Buck and Aunt Lizzie as long as I could. Soon, dust hid them from my sight.

Chapter 8

It was Saturday, parade day, and I was up at six o'clock. I looked out the kitchen window toward the woods. The leaves on the aspen trees were twisting on their stems and glittering in the morning sunlight. When the wind blows into those trees they sparkle like sequins.

I still had a little work to do on my plan. Mom and Dad were sleeping in like they usually do on Saturday mornings. I quickly got one of the paint tubes from Mom's art supplies. Black would be good I decided, and the one-inch paintbrush from the workroom was just right. They fit nicely into the pocket of my new buckskin shirt. I pulled on my moccasins and the old Davy Crockett pants from Grandma's attic, slipped the new shirt over my head, and fastened the rawhide laces. The coonskin hat was the finishing touch. I looked and felt like a frontier hero.

Outside in the backyard, the wind caught the fringe of my shirt. It twisted and danced around in the sunlight like the aspen leaves. I held up my arms and the leaves and fringe twisted at the same time. I scouted around in the woods to get in the pioneer mood. In the moccasins I could easily feel the ground beneath my feet as I walked. Even the smallest sticks, leaves, and pebbles could be felt through the bottoms. It was a lot like being barefoot and I felt light on my feet. But I wasn't as quiet as I thought I would be wearing moccasins. There were old dry leaves all over the ground and wherever I stepped I rustled and crumbled leaves. Birds screeched and squirrels chit-chatted about the noisy human who was squashing his way through their woods. I would have to find out how Indians were able to move so quietly through the woods that they could sneak up behind a bear and whack him on the backside. I heard they could do that.

The longer I walked, the quieter I got. I watched where my feet were about to step down, and tried not to step on anything I didn't have to. I found that stepping on rocks is really quiet, and that, if I slipped my toes under the leaves before stepping down, I didn't make nearly as much noise. It seemed like the quieter I got, the less I was there in the woods. I stood on a big silver rock to listen and watch. I felt invisible, like I was just these two ears and eyes listening and watching. Some time passed and then a jet roared overhead. Suddenly, I was aware of where I was again. I checked my watch and, seeing the time, I ran back to the house.

We took three pictures before we left—one of Dad and me, one of Mom and me in front of the woodpile, and one of me standing by the wheelbarrow. A car honked as it drove by. It was pretty embarrassing. Mom said that I had better get used to it because there would be a lot more before the day was over.

Dad, Sandy, and I drove downtown to the starting point of the parade. We arrived a little early so Dad walked over to some booths to get information about other things going on that day. Sandy and I walked around the float a couple times. Once was not enough to take it all in. It looked something like a three-layer wedding cake. Sitting on the top layer was Miss Stillwater. Sandy said I should climb up to say hello. Miss Stillwater was wearing an Indian princess costume and she had the shiniest, whitest teeth I have ever seen. Her eyes were dark and twinkly. She was so pretty that when she talked to me, I didn't hear what she said for a few seconds. She said her name was Mickey something. Mickey seemed like a strange name for a girl. I found out later it was really Michelle. Mickey and I were supposed to sit together on a bench on top of the float.

Meanwhile, Sandy was standing in front of the float watching a man from the city vacuum off cobwebs from under the stuffed bear's arms and from between the bear's teeth. When the guy started vacuuming cobwebs from between Snuffy's legs, some of the Boy Scouts, who were watching, howled as if the bear were crying out in pain. Sandy rolled her eyes and walked away.

Now it was time to get my plan rolling, because the cars were starting and the bands were lining up.

I waved to Sandy to come to the top of the float where I was sitting.

"Sandy, what are you doing for the next two hours?"

"What? I'm going to watch the parade with Mom and Dad and Tommy, and then I'm going to play bingo. Why?"

"Well," I hesitated, "I want you to ride up here with me."

"Are you crazy? No. . . . No! I'm getting down." She hopped down to the next tier.

"Wait!" I shouted, before she went any farther. "You belong up here, too. You're just as much a hero as me. You almost got yourself killed running alongside that car the way you did."

"I'm not supposed to be up here. It's for you, not me." Sandy turned around again.

"Listen, Sandy." The band began its first number. "If you don't get up here and ride in this parade, I'm getting down, too." I hopped down with her and waited. It was her turn to make a move.

She gritted her teeth and squinted at me. "No way. I mean it. No way." I hopped down to the first tier. She seemed to be getting weaker. "Besides," she added, "I don't even have a costume, or anything. And look at that sign. It has your name on it. If I'm up here people will say, 'Who's that up there? What's she doing on the float? Get her off.'"

"Well, that's not a problem. Just watch this." I pulled out the paint and paintbrush and began to change the sign. I drew a big arrow from the word "hero" down to the words "Sandy Larson," which I added. Then under my name I wrote the words "quick thinker." So the sign ended up looking like this:

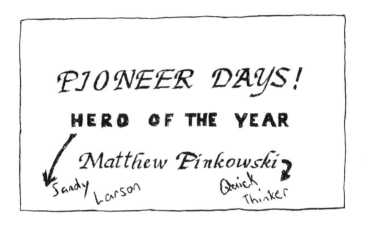

I spelled everything right. I had asked Mom how to spell Sandy's name and even looked up "quick" and "thinker" in the dictionary. Sandy's mouth was open about as far as Snuffy's, except she looked more surprised than ferocious. Before she could get her mouth closed, I put Uncle Buck's coonskin cap on her head and pulled out Dad's little raggy one from under my buckskin shirt for me. Sandy finally laughed, because the hat I was wearing sat way up on top of my head, instead of down over it.

Next, I introduced Sandy to Mickey. "Mickey, this is my friend Sandy. She's a hero, too." Then I turned toward Sandy. "Sandy, this is Mickey. She goes to college in Mankato." Mickey and Sandy hit it off just fine. The float started to pull away just as Dad came back. When he saw the sign, he spilled orange pop all over his white golf shirt.

The three of us sat looking out over Snuffy's freshly vacuumed body. The rest of our float was full of people.

All around the bottom layer, except in the front, were Boy Scouts dressed like Indians. In the front was Snuffy. He stood on his hind legs with his front legs and claws reaching out to rip up whatever was in front of him. His mouth was open in a huge, snarling growl. He looked like something I had seen in my nightmares. Several little kids went crying to their mothers when Snuffy came by.

On the second layer were the girls from Madame Monique's Ballet and Tap Dancing Studio. They were dressed up like Indian maidens, except for their black tap shoes, red lipstick, and white gloves. Those girls could really smile—every one of them. I watched to see if they could keep it up for the whole parade. It turned out they could. They also waved better than anyone I had ever seen. They used that side-to-side wave that I've seen people use in the Rose Bowl parade on TV. Those Madame Monique girls sat with their legs folded perfectly, smiling and waving their side-to-side waves for two solid hours, and only one of them ever broke ranks. I think she had to use the bathroom, because she bolted off the float and right through the crowd into McGuigan's Drug Store. She didn't get back on the float until two blocks later.

"Where'd you go?" one of the scouts asked her. He laughed and eyed his buddy.

She gave him a lightning kick with a tap-shoe toe to his kneecap. Before he knew what hit him, he fell over holding his knee and almost cried. Madame Monique must teach a little karate in her dance classes.

The Boy Scouts couldn't sit as still as Madame Monique's girls. They waved all wrong and wore out their waves after about three blocks. Each scout had a little bag of candy to throw to the little kids. Some did, but some ate their candy and some threw it at older kids in the crowd who made faces at them. When the parade ended at Pioneer Park, the scout leader lectured the Boy Scouts about pride and behavior and the traditions of scouting.

Pioneer Park is a picnic place at the top of the bluff on the north side of town. From there, you can see all of Stillwater, which stretches from the top of the bluff right down to the St. Croix River. It's a great view. Most of the rooftops are hidden beneath elm and cottonwood trees. I counted seven church steeples of different sizes and shapes pointed toward the sky like the lightning rods on Uncle Buck's barn. I could see cars waiting in the heat to go across the Stillwater bridge. It was raised for a big boat to pass under.

Pioneer Park has a one-lane road running through it. The road is like the ones running through graveyards in small towns. Cars drive in, curve around a horseshoe-shaped turn, and come out a little further down the park road. It reminds me of a cemetery, except there are picnic tables instead of gravestones and people fool around instead of being respectful.

Sandy, at the first chance, said a polite Thank-you and scaled down the tiers of the float to the ground. She disappeared into the crowd, thinking she was safe.

Mickey and I made our way to the bandstand for the ceremony and speeches. We sat on some metal folding chairs along with a bunch of other people I didn't know. Everybody looked calm and smiley except me. I tried to smile like everybody else, but I'm sure only the corners of my mouth curved up. The rest of my face looked as scared as I was.

A radio announcer from Minneapolis started the program and introduced people. He told some good jokes about small towns that the crowd really liked. He was a good speaker, and it was fun listening to him. I didn't realize how good he was until the mayor got up to talk.

Mayor Richert was a tap-and-blow-in-the-micro-phone sort of speaker. He got that microphone to do some squeals I had never heard before. The mayor began by clearing his throat into the microphone. "Can everyone out there hear me?" I remember thinking that the only people who could possibly say No must have a hearing problem.

He talked about "this fair city," and "founding fathers," and a little about the "pioneer spirit." "Our

—46—

founding fathers began this fair city one hundred and fifty years ago. They possessed a pioneer spirit that we honor here today." The audience clapped politely when he finished, and then came back to life when the radio announcer returned and told a funny joke about a mayor.

Next came the bouquet of roses for Mickey. She said a few words about being glad to be there and it being an honor.

Mickey was followed by a general or something from the VFW—that's Veterans of Foreign Wars. I'm not sure what they do, but they're in a lot of parades. They're men of all different ages and they wear army uniforms. I think they run a building for wedding receptions, but I don't know what that has to do with army uniforms. He used a lot of the same lines that the mayor had used. The general spoke with his hands on his hips and talked about fighting men and the flag and about vets. I clapped loudly for him when he was done, mostly because it seemed like the right thing to do.

Mr. Duncan was next. He was the man who had called Mom. Mr. Duncan looked about as old as my dad, which is pretty old. He looked over the crowd and walked up to the microphone. "As you all know, each year the Stillwater Chamber of Commerce recognizes the person in the community who most represents the pioneer qualities of selfless bravery. This year we bestow the honor on a young man who single-handedly saved the life of one of his neighbors. I be-

—47—

lieve almost everyone here is familiar with the story from reading about it in the newspaper and seeing it on the TV news. Ladies and gentlemen, I want you to meet this young man. Matthew Pinkowski, come on up here."

Loud clapping and some whistles came from the people crowded around the bandstand. I was so scared my legs shook the whole way to the microphone. Mickey gave me a big shiny smile and said, "Don't be nervous." That was easy for her to say. She was already finished talking at the microphone.

Mr. Duncan leaned down and shook my hand. "Congratulations, Matthew."

"Thank you, Mr. Duncan." I said somehow.

I think Mr. Duncan knew I was nervous and tried to help, but he didn't succeed. "Say Matthew, who was that attractive young lady with you on the float?"

"Oh," I answered. "That was Mickey, I mean Michelle Filben, Miss Stillwater. That's her over there." I pointed to Mickey.

"No, no, no," he said. "The other attractive young lady sitting next to you."

My brain went blank for a few seconds. Then I remembered.

"Oh, you mean Sandy?" The crowd laughed really hard at that, although I wasn't trying to be funny.

"Sandy?" he said. "Is that your girlfriend?"

"No," I said. "Well, she's my friend and she, she's a girl, so I guess she's a girl friend but *not* my girl-friend." My face was really hot.

"Matthew," Mr. Duncan asked, "if she's not your girlfriend, then whose girlfriend is she?"

"I don't think she is one, Mr. Duncan."

He put his arm around me, brought me close to the microphone, and whispered, "I think you'd better find out in a hurry." He laughed along with the rest of the crowd. I was really embarrassed. There's a friend of my parents who always teases me about liking girls and he can really embarrass me. I don't know why people get such a charge out of embarrassing boys about girls.

"Sandy is my friend," I said into the microphone. "I asked her to come on the float with me because she tried to save Tommy's life, too. Only she couldn't. She cut her knees trying, and I thought she was very brave. I tricked her to get her onto the float. She didn't want to be there." Everyone, including Mr. Duncan, became quiet.

After a couple of seconds, Mr. Duncan said something about that being big of me. Then he said, "Say, let's get your friend Sandy up here, too. If you like, you can read her name along with yours when you read the plaque."

I had seen Sandy standing near the back of the crowd with her mom and dad. I looked just in time to see Sandy sneak behind a big oak tree so no one would see her. I leaned up to the microphone and pointed to the tree. "I just saw her go behind that big oak." There was a lot of commotion and heads turning. Sandy's dad disappeared behind the tree and came back around pulling Sandy by the wrist. Everybody clapped as she was led up to the stage by her dad.

Poor Sandy didn't know what to do. She walked over by me, frowned, and squinted a lot. Mr. Duncan got the plaque. Sandy leaned over and whispered something. I thought she was going to whisper Thanks. Instead she whispered, "I'm going to kill you just as soon as we're alone."

Mr. Duncan returned with the plaque. He shook Sandy's hand. "Hello, Sandy. Congratulations to you, too. Matthew says you are a brave young woman. What do you think about that?"

"I don't know. I tried, but I couldn't help too much. Matthew's the one who stopped the car."

"Well, aren't these a couple of fine young people we have here for Pioneer Days? Let's have a big hand for both of them."

Mr. Duncan then held the plaque out for me. "Matthew, I'd like you to read this plaque, presented to you on behalf of the Stillwater Chamber of Commerce."

I took the plaque in my hand and stared at it for what seemed like ten minutes. I knew the first word—it was "this." As far as the rest of the words went, I had never seen such long words before. At school, Ms. Schmidke helped me get started and wouldn't laugh or rush me if I made a mistake. My face got so hot that it started to sting. Sometimes I make pretty good guesses at words because they fit in with what I was reading. I had never gotten a plaque before so I wasn't sure what these words sounded like.

I wasn't about to say to all those people that I couldn't read it. I knew that no one out in the audience had much of an idea what was on the plaque. I hoped Mr. Duncan wouldn't say anything. This is how it came out: "This plaque . . . um, pretty to . . . stirring pony . . . no pion . . . Pioneer Days . . .

"Mr. Duncan," I blurted out, "I'm a little nervous. Maybe you'd better read it for me."

"Sure, sure, I don't blame you. There's only about a thousand people out there." He took the plaque from me.

"This plaque is presented to the Stillwater Pioneer Days Hero of the Year, Matthew Pinkowski, for outstanding, selfless effort in the quest to preserve human life and well being."

"And Sandy Larson," I added quickly.

"Yes, and Sandy Larson," he added. The crowd clapped and smiled.

Chapter 9

I thanked Mr. Duncan, shook his hand, and re-treated to my seat as fast as I could. I was relieved to be off center stage. It was the same feeling I get when I leave the dentist's office.

Next Mrs. Houlee, from the roller rink, who also plays organ at the Lutheran church, played some songs that sounded a lot like some I remember hearing on my grandma's radio. Some people stayed and sang along while others mosied off to play bingo or go to the beer garden. Mr. Duncan came back on stage and thanked everybody in town, one by one, for "all their help in making it the biggest and best Pioneer Days ever."

I made my way down the wooden stage steps and across the trampled grass to my family. Dad held out his hand. "Good job, son. Your mother and I are very proud." Dad shook my hand just the way he does when he meets grown-up people. He looks them straight in the eye and shakes their hand like he means it.

"Thanks, Dad," I said, smiling. As much as Dad could make me feel grown-up, Mom's hug and kiss made me feel like a little kid again. I'm not sure which way of being treated I like better. Maybe it's all part of the territory when you're thirteen.

Pretty soon Sandy and I got tired of all the compliments and pats on the back. I signaled Tommy, and the three of us made off for where an old man near the edge of the bluff had set up a telescope. The man was tall, with thin tufts of white hair that moved easily in the breeze. He wore tinted glasses that didn't go very well with blue eyes. His glasses sat on a large nose and his mouth was a little open all the time like he was always just a bit out of breath. His arms and legs looked heavy, but the rest of him was pretty lean. His hands were thick like a carpenter's.

A little hand-painted sign leaned against the legs of the tripod. It said 25¢ A Minute. We all had some money, so we each bought ourselves a minute.

"Do you have change for a dollar, mister?" asked Tommy.

"Sure do. Come on up here. You ever look in a telescope before?"

"No."

"Well then, did you ever look through a pair of binoculars?" The old man held up his hands as if he were holding a pair of binoculars.

"Oh, those." Tommy reached into his back pocket and pulled out one-half of a pair of binoculars.

The man lifted his eyebrows in surprise. "Just happened to have a binocular with you, huh?" Tommy nodded.

"Sure, they're pretty near the same thing, only the telescope's bigger."

Sandy told me the binocular had been in a junk box in their attic. About once a week Tommy went up there and found something. Then he carried it around in his pocket until he got tired of it.

The man set a little egg timer for one minute and Tommy stepped up to the telescope for a look. Tommy looked with both eyes open. Even though the man told him to close one eye, Tommy didn't seem to be able to do it. I know that you have to close one eye because otherwise your brain gets mixed up with two different pictures.

I began to see what Sandy had said about Tommy's asking questions. When he found he wasn't seeing much, he started asking questions instead. "Where'd you get this telescope? These telescopes cost a lot, don't they? A periscope's not the same as a telescope, is it? Do people still use submarines? Where do you live? Where's your mother?" The man answered all of Tommy's questions.

Finally Sandy cut in, "Tommy, your minute is gonna be up in about two seconds, so look!" The bell went off just as Tommy got back up to the telescope.

"Here, take another few seconds," the man said, waving his hand at the timer. "The line's not too long."

"Tommy," Sandy said. "Cover one eye with your hand if you can't do it the other way."

"Oh, now I see! There's somebody walking down the sidewalk. They're looking right at me."

"Come on, Tommy, let somebody else have a turn," I said.

Sandy paid her quarter and began her turn by looking down the river toward the bridge. Then she aimed the telescope toward the bluff farther down river. "I'm going to try to see our house from here." She moved the telescope back and forth and up and down. "Let's see. There's the turret on the Jacob's old place. That's down the hill where the road turns. No, too many trees. I can see where it's supposed to be, but all the houses and garages are out of sight. Too many dumb trees." She pulled her head away from the telescope and squinted, looking in the same direction.

"What is it?" I asked.

"Just a second," she said, looking through the telescope. "You know what? I think I see a hole or a cave in the side of the bluff, and it looks like it's pretty close to our houses. There are trees in front of it, but from this angle, it's easy to see it—at least with a telescope it is."

"Let me see," I said excitedly.

"Just a second. Just a second. Mister, can you adjust this a little bit? It's still a little bit blurry."

Just then the bell went off. "My turn! Excuse me ma'am," I said, crowding Sandy's head away as I moved mine in place. I found the spot right away. "Yeah, I see it. I wonder if anyone has ever seen it before. It's really well hidden."

As the old man showed me where to adjust the eyepiece, he said, "I've been living in Stillwater my whole life and I know there are caves around. The Indians used them for big meetings. Later on the white man came along and used the caves for storing things — mostly beer and ammunition. Most of the other caves around these parts have been cemented up. If there's a cave on that bluff, it's not one I've ever heard of."

There didn't seem to be any paths leading to the cave that I could see. In fact, it didn't look like a person could climb up to it because the rock wall was so steep. About twenty feet from the top there was a grassy area with a lot of trees and bushes scattered over it. The area created was like a huge step. About fifteen feet deep, it began at a steep rock that came up from the valley floor, and ended at another steep wall of limestone that continued twenty feet or so to the top.

"We should try to find it," I said. "It looks like it's straight down from the houses in our neighborhood. Wouldn't it be exciting?"

Sandy looked a little worried. "How would we get to it? We aren't mountain climbers, you know."

"Oh, don't worry so much. There's got to be a way to get to it."

"I guess so," Sandy said slowly. "It's just that one close call is enough for the summer. It sure doesn't look like anyone could get to it." The bell went off, so I turned the telescope away from the hill so no other kids would find our cave.

When the next kid started his turn, I asked the man, "What do you do with this telescope? Do you watch boats from up here, or spy on people, or what?"

He laughed so that part of his smile disappeared under his nose. "No, no. I only use it at night. My wife, Mert, and I live over there in that corner house. She don't get around so good anymore, so we got ourselves a new hobby last spring. Every clear night we go out on the front porch, turn off all the house lights, and gaze up at the heavens. There's a lot up there to see."

"Like what?" I asked. "Stars?"

"Yes, and much, much more. Last week, we saw the eclipse of the moon. The week before that we saw a shower of falling stars. They looked like a flock of fireflies all racing around in the sky. Have you kids ever seen the northern lights, the Aurora Borealis?"

"What's that?" Tommy asked.

"The Aurora Borealis is a glowing arch of light that points to the North Pole. You can only see it on certain nights when the conditions are just right. When the sun gets really active, it shoots charged particles into space. When the little particles get close to earth, they glow.

"Maybe my explanation was a little confusing, but you don't have to understand the northern lights to enjoy them. Well, for that matter, maybe they're easier to enjoy if you don't understand. I guess they're more of a wonder then. Anyway, they can give you goose bumps and make you feel small as a baby. There aren't many things that can make you feel that way when you're my age." He looked off at the sky over the city and smiled to himself. He wasn't listening when Tommy asked another question.

"How come you're letting kids look in your telescope?"

"What? Oh, to help pay for the telescope."

"Mister," Sandy asked, "can you really see all that stuff you were talking about from your front porch?"

"Yes, especially in the spring before the leaves come out. Our neighbors were even nice enough to trim some of the branches off the maple in the front yard so we could see better."

"That's pretty neat," Sandy said with a serious look on her face. "I used to like reading about stars and planets and constellations, but I never could find much in the sky besides the moon and the Big Dipper."

Tommy quickly replied, "How about the sun, Sandy? Don't you ever see the sun?" Tommy was grinning widely. Sandy rolled her eyes.

"Mister," Sandy said, changing the subject, "what's your name? We know your wife's name and she's not even here."

"Jenkins. Alfred A. Jenkins. I don't believe I caught your names, either." We told him our names and he said he knew Mrs. Larson from a church committee some years ago.

Sandy continued, "Mr. Jenkins, tell us some more about the things you see from the front porch." Mr. Jenkins looked down at his boots for a few seconds and then looked up again.

"Did you children know that you can see the colors of stars with a telescope?" We shook our heads.

"Sure thing. Some of them are red, some blue, and some yellow."

"I didn't know that," Tommy said flatly. "How come they're different colors?"

"Different colors from different temperatures. Some of the stars burn hotter than others so they give off different colors." He paused and looked across the river at the sky above the Wisconsin bluffs. "You know, the sky is a wonderful place to travel. It is so big. I only wish I had started to learn about it sooner." He turned around and squinted up at the sun. "Oh, well."

Then Mr. Jenkins gazed back at us. "Say, you kids seem interested. I'll tell you something. Read books. Ask questions. There's so much to learn, and you can learn it all. Don't waste time. There's not as much of it as you think."

There was sadness in his voice as he spoke to us. It felt like it was our fault somehow that we had more time to learn things than he did. We didn't say anything, just watched the ground and fiddled around with the stones at our feet.

"Say, listen to old man Jenkins talk on," he said. "I'll bet that's why you kids came over here, to get a good lecture, right? Mertle says sometimes I ramble on a bit."

"Mom says I ramble on, too," Tommy replied. "She says, 'Zip that lip.'" What Tommy was saying sounded like a wise-guy thing to say, but Mr. Jenkins knew he didn't mean it that way. You can tell with Tommy.

A quality that I like in Tommy is that he doesn't beat around the bush when he wants to say something. Usually, if you want to come over to someone's house, you say something like, "Hey, we should get together sometime. By the way, you have a really nice house. What do you say?"

Not Tommy, though. He just comes right out with it. "Can we all come over to your house tonight and look through your telescope, Mr. Jenkins?"

Tommy was as surprised as Sandy and I were when he agreed.

Mr. and Mrs. Larson dropped us off at the Jenkins's house about eight o'clock that night. Mrs. Larson knew Mr. and Mrs. Jenkins pretty well and assured my mom and dad that it would be all right to leave us there for a couple hours. The Larsons were on their way to the big street dance on Main Street. A whole block had been roped off. All over town you could hear the oom-paa music, with accordians and all. It's the type of music my parents like, too. They tell me they had lots of it at their wedding. I've seen pictures of them dancing the polka at their wedding. Mom looked the same then, only she was a little skinnier and her lips were redder. Dad's hair was really short, and it made his ears look big.

The sun was just about down and the tall shadows from the houses poured across the front lawns, down the steep banks, across the sidewalks, and into the street. When we hopped out of the car, I could see the sun shining right through the Jenkins's house. It came through a back window and shone out one of the front windows. The shadow from the house lay out in the street, and it had a window in it, too.

I was the first one up the steps. I knocked extra loud in case they were hard of hearing, like Uncle Buck. "Hello, hello, hello," Mr. Jenkins said opening the door. "Come right on in. I was just cleaning the lens of the telescope. Go right into the living room. Mertle is in there doing something or other.

"Mert," he called, "the kids from the park are here."

Our tennis shoes squeaked across the dark wooden floorboards as we made our way into the living room. It was a large, well-lit room with a high ceiling, wide, dark woodwork, and four or five faded, squashed-out-of-shape, stuffed chairs. The chairs were set in a half circle facing the fireplace. But instead of a fire in there, there was a small TV set. It was sitting right in the fireplace.

Mrs. Jenkins sat in the high-backed chair nearest the fireplace. "You kids will have to excuse me for not getting up, but at my age a body's just got so many get-ups left in it. C'mon over and set yourselves down. We'll get to the who's who in a minute here. Al, would you get the kids some iced tea? You kids drink iced tea, don't you?"

"Oh, yes," I said politely. "It's quite refreshing." I had never had any before, so this was my chance. Sandy and Tommy said No, thank-you, so they got ginger ale instead.

The old chairs were really comfortable. There were hollows in them from where people must have sat over the years.

Mr. Jenkins called from the kitchen. "Mert, where's the tea?"

"It's right where it has been for the last fifty-two years—in the cupboard above the sink."

"Well, it ain't there now. I just looked."

"I can see I'm gonna have to use one of my get-ups now." She pushed herself slowly off the chair and closed her eyes once like something hurt. She slowly straightened up as she made her way to the kitchen.

There were large windows in the living room that came almost to the floor. They opened to the porch, which let in a cooling breeze that blew the bottom half of the silky white curtains around making them look like angel dresses. Inside the living room, the walls were covered with faded wallpaper that had ivy vines and pink flowers wandering all over it. I don't know why, but older people's houses are quiet. My grandma's house is the same way. You can always hear clocks ticking on end tables or fireplace mantels. Besides the ticking clock, above the fireplace, were several old pictures of people who I figured must be relatives. There were pictures of women in nurse's outfits, men with short haircuts in army uniforms, young people in graduation gowns, and couples at their weddings. The wedding pictures looked just like my parent's—pretty women and guys with big ears. I didn't see any pictures of kids, maybe because kids don't wear uniforms that much, or maybe the Jenkinses never had any.

Mrs. Jenkins came in carrying a serving tray holding four clinking glasses and a mug of beer. She set the tray on the coffee table and picked up the beer for herself. Tommy drank his ginger ale without stopping. I learned I didn't like iced tea.

"You musta been pretty refreshed before you started drinking there, young fella," said Mrs. Jenkins, smiling. "You barely tasted your tea."

"Yes. Pretty refreshed," I replied, realizing she knew I didn't like it.

"By the way," she continued, looking at my buckskin outfit, "what are you dressed up like that for? Animal skins and furry hats were just going out of style when I was a little girl. Is that what young boys are wearing today?" She looked over at Mr. Jenkins. "Alfred, you gotta get me outta this house more often. I think I'm back in style again."

Mr. Jenkins seemed impatient. "No, Mert. That's his outfit for Pioneer Days! Matthew here was the Pioneer Days' hero this year. Remember?"

"Is that so?" she asked, raising her eyebrows. "What'd you do? Wrestle a bear or something?"

Mr. Jenkins cut in, "Mert, you remember. I told you about the boy who dumped over the logs to stop the runaway car."

"You're him?" she asked, sounding surprised. "I had you pictured a might bigger. Oh, well, you don't have to be big to have guts." She thought for a few seconds, extended her hand and said, "Glad to meet you, Matthew." She also shook Tommy and Sandy's hands and asked their names. We answered the usual grown-up questions about what grade we were in, how many brothers and sisters we had, and where we lived. We found out that the Jenkinses had only one son, who had been killed in a war somewhere. He was one of the army guys on the fireplace mantel.

It wasn't long until we brought the telescope out on the porch. It was nice to be able to look without having to pay a quarter or be finished in one minute. First we viewed the moon, which was about half full

and just rising above the Wisconsin side of the river. The telescope was so powerful that the whole moon couldn't even fit in it. I wasn't sure what I was looking at for a couple seconds. When I got things in focus, the hills and craters jumped out at me.

Next we sighted in on the stars. We saw the colors in the stars just as Mr. Jenkins had said we would. There were more of them than I had thought. I remembered when our fourth-grade teacher read us *The Little House on the Prairie*, and how Laura camped with her family out in their covered wagon. She had said she watched the stars at night, just as we were doing. She said they seemed so close and so large that she felt she could almost reach out and pluck them from the sky. I understood what she meant. Using a telescope, though, made me feel like I was floating right up in the sky with the stars.

About eleven o'clock, Mr. Larson called to say he'd be by soon to pick us up. While the three of us sat waiting on the squeaky porch swing, Mrs. Jenkins leaned forward on her chair and said to me, "Do you know who was the bravest person I ever knew?" I didn't, so I shook my head. "It was my older sister Molly."

"Why," I asked, "did she save somebody, too?"

"No, not exactly. Way back in the early thirties, she and her young husband were farming. They had three little children under the age of seven. She was still nursing the baby when one day her young husband, a big galoot of a man, was killed when a big load of lumber slid off a wagon right on top of him. Mercy Mary! You talk about sad."

"What'd she do all by herself?" Sandy wanted to know.

"I came home with her that night and watched the little ones for her. The poor thing, all through the night she cried and moaned and cried some more. She cursed that man for getting himself killed and then cried some more out of shame. She must have cried away most of the hurt. Next morning she came out of that bedroom looking like a horse had just dragged her halfway across the county. Her jaw and mouth, though, were set like stone as she came over, hugged each of them children, got herself dressed, and walked out, saying she'd be back before lunch."

"Where'd she go?" Tommy asked.

"She rode right over to the orphanage in Rochester and arranged to adopt a strong fourteen-year-old girl named Elizabeth. Molly promised she'd send her to college some day if she'd be part of the family and mind the children. That afternoon Molly asked a neighbor to show her how to use the tractor, and before the week was out, Molly had the corn crop in the ground herself.

"She ran that place for five years and showed a profit the last three. Then she met a seed salesman from Winona. She got married and things eased up a lot."

"Did Elizabeth go with them?" Sandy asked.

"Oh, yes. They got her all caught up in school and sent her to the big university over in Minneapolis.

She studied old bones or something. I guess she was pretty good at it because she wrote a book about it. Why anybody'd ever want to read about bones is beyond me, but they say she done it. That Molly was a brave woman."

"Mert," said Mr. Jenkins, "it seems to me there are maybe two kinds of courage—daring and determination. That's it. Matthew here had daring. Molly had determination."

Mrs. Jenkins said, "Yeah, I suppose that's true." She seemed far away.

Mr. Larson drove up in his car. Tommy jumped off the swing and waved. Everybody said good-bye about five times, and we kids said thank-you at least that many times.

As we headed down the steps that night, Mr. Jenkins stopped Tommy and poked him several times in the chest saying, "Young man, you keep right on asking those questions. That's the way you learn. I like to see it. You keep it up."

Tommy grinned and answered, "Yes, sir." Mr. Jenkins slapped him on the back and the three of us went down to the waiting car.

The short drive home was quiet. It was a nice change from a day that had been anything but quiet. I remember thinking that the rest of the summer was going to seem pretty dull. Was I ever wrong.

Chapter 10

I stayed in bed until eleven. During the night, a storm had blown in and it rained right into the morning. The cooler air and the steady, plunking sound of the rain on the window made me feel all the more sleepy. Every so often I could hear thunder in the distance. It seemed to say, "Pull the covers up a little higher and go back to sleep."

The thunder was far away at first. It sounded like the soft purring of a cat. After a while the thunder came closer and closer and began to sound like cracks from a circus whip. Every time the thunder cracked, the rain seemed to fall harder, as if the thunder were shaking extra rain out of the clouds.

I finally got out of bed, got dressed, and ate some Cheerios. Mom waved to me while she was talking on the phone. She whispered that it was Grandpa, so I knew she would talk about an hour.

I put on my orange rain poncho and headed for the Larson's. The sidewalks were full of worms and the air was full of the smell of rain. I sloshed over to see if Tommy and Sandy were doing anything interesting. I found the two of them reading on their back porch.

"Hey, you two bookworms, let's go look for the cave."

I must have startled them because they jumped, and Tommy's magazine fell onto the floor. Sandy sat back down and sighed, "In case you didn't notice, it's raining out. See? Water drops—H_2O. Makes you wet."

"So what? You won't melt. Skin is pretty much waterproof, I've heard. There are some new inventions you'll have to check out, too. They're called umbrellas and raincoats."

Both Sandy and Tommy are "doing" kids, not the sit-around type. Before long, we were near the edge of the bluff behind the house two houses up from the Larson's. It was our best guess as to where we had seen the cave.

"Don't go near the edge!" Tommy warned. "You might fall."

We were about twenty feet from the edge, and Tommy was already nervous. Tommy stayed back because he wasn't sure of his balance. And he could fall. I'd seen him trip over branches and curbs that other kids wouldn't have any trouble with. Sandy and I walked carefully until we were about four or five feet from the edge of the cliff. We lay down on the tall grass and slid slowly forward until we could just peek over the edge.

The drop was about twenty feet straight down. Then there was the narrow band of woods running along the cliff wall for about two hundred yards. Just below that the cliff dropped down to another small woods that bordered some backyards.

"We can't see the cave from here," I said. We'll have to go down below. Then we can walk along the ledge and find the cave with no sweat."

"How do you think you're going to get down there without killing yourself?" Sandy wanted to know.

"I don't know, but don't worry. Come on, let's walk down a ways and see if we can't find a way to get to that woodsy patch."

The three of us made our way downriver, high-stepping through the wild grasses growing at the edge of the bluff. The legs of our jeans were soaked and they stuck to our legs. Soon we got to a spot where the top of the cliff was only ten feet or so from the woodsy patch. There was a warped and twisted old oak tree in the patch. Some of its branches reached up to the bluff. It really seemed too good to be true, but then so does Christmas.

It wouldn't be too dangerous for Sandy or me to climb down, but there was no way Tommy was going to be able to do it. "You guys better not go down there. You'll fall," Tommy said, in a soft, serious voice.

"Tommy, I climb up and down trees all the time," Sandy said. "This is no more dangerous than the trees in our backyard. In fact, the grass down below looks a lot softer than our backyard. Don't worry, Tommy." Sandy hopped up onto the branch and began sliding toward the tree trunk, where the branch is strongest. When she got safely to another branch, I followed her.

The trick to climbing is where you look. If you look all the way to the bottom, you get scared, because you know you are really a long way up. But if you just watch the branch you're on, it's a cinch. You could walk up and down a branch all day if it's sitting on the ground and you'd never fall off. Just looking at the branch fools you into thinking you're on the ground.

The branches going down the trunk were well-spaced, so it was easy to get down. At the bottom we had a little four-foot jump, but that wasn't any problem. We looked through the rain at the cliff above us. Tommy was out of sight, far back from the edge of the drop-off.

"We made it, Tommy," I hollered. "No sweat."

"Can you see the cave?" he shouted back.

"Not from here," Sandy yelled. "We'll have to walk upriver a ways."

Sandy and I worked our way back along the wide ledge toward where we thought the cave would be. We called back and forth to Tommy so he could keep pace with us. We had walked for about two hundred yards when Tommy called from above.

"This is the place where you guys looked down before. I can see where you were laying in the grass. Do you see anything?"

"No," I called back. "Wait a second!" I ran over a few steps. "There it is!"

"Do you see any bears in there?" Tommy yelled. "You gotta watch out for bears. They like caves."

The entrance to the cave was eight to ten feet above us. Sandy was taking a good look around an aspen tree that partly covered the entrance. She hopped up, grabbed a limb, and swung her feet up to the branch. With a lot of kicking and swinging, she got herself sitting on the branch. Sandy chose two or three more branches and reached, pulled, and stepped her way up to the cave entrance. Swinging from the springy aspen branch she stood in the cave, just out of sight.

I called up to Tommy. "She's in the cave, Tommy. She made it."

"Sandy, what's it like?" I asked from below. "Do you see any tracks or anything?"

"No, just sand. It doesn't look like it goes back very far."

From up above Tommy shouted words of warning. "Watch out for cave-ins. Caves are always caving in."

"Don't worry, Tommy," Sandy called back. "It looks really sturdy."

I followed Sandy's route up the tree. Within a couple minutes we were looking the cave over. The entrance was under a little overhang about seven feet high. Near the edges it was lower, and I bumped my head really hard. The opening was about ten feet wide, so with the sloping edges it looked like a half-moon turned on its side.

Just inside, the floor was covered with a yellowish, sandy powder. The walls and ceiling were made out of the same stuff, which we later found out was limestone. The cave was a little bigger once we were inside, but it got smaller fast. It was only about twelve feet deep. Way in the back there was a musty smell, like my Grandma Mary's basement. There was a quietness about the cave that made it a little spooky and a little exciting, too.

Walking back to the entrance, we had a terrific view. Through the tops of the aspen trees we could see all the way to Pioneer Park. The steeples and treetops of Stillwater were right below us. Beyond flowed the St. Croix River, looking gray and cold on this rainy day. Below and off to our right was Highway 95, winding along the river from Bayport. Above the aspen tops stretched as much sky as you would ever need to look at. Today it looked as gray, cold, and wet as the river below.

The cave was perfect. It was hard enough to get to, but not too hard. And the view was great. I leaned out the entrance and howled. "Whoo-eee!"

Tommy shouted from above, "What's wrong?"

"Nothing! It's perfect."

"You've got to see it," Sandy added.

"No, I might fall."

Sandy wrinkled her nose because she knew Tommy was right. He couldn't climb trees, at least not without falling half the time. I couldn't think of any way for him to get to the cave. At least then I couldn't. I was so excited about our cave that I wasn't really thinking much about anyone else's problems.

It was starting to rain harder, with lightning and thunder. Sandy and I wiggled down the aspen tree, ran back through the wet grass, and climbed the oak tree to the top of the bluff where Tommy was waiting. On the way back to the house, we agreed we'd better not tell our parents about the cave. We knew enough about parents to know that they would say the cave was too dangerous. We knew it wasn't, though.

Tommy was full of questions about the cave. Sandy had taught me that it was not a good idea to answer more than one or two of Tommy's questions at a time, otherwise he'd never stop asking. But this time Sandy and I answered every one of them. Two adventures in one summer were too good to be true.

Chapter 11

We left our wet shoes on the back porch at the Larson's house. Mrs. Larson let me wear a pair of Tommy's sweatpants because my jeans were soaked past the knee from the wet grass. I joined Sandy and Tommy in the kitchen where they were putting cheese sandwiches together. We watched an old Tarzan movie on a little TV in the kitchen and the three of us whispered a lot about the cave until Mrs. Larson reminded us that whispering is not polite.

I talked Sandy and Tommy into playing a game I used to play with my friends in St. Paul. You turn down the TV sound and make up things for the people in the show to say. I was Tarzan. Sandy was Jane and Tommy played Mr. Richardson, a reporter.

Tarzan:	Mr. Richardson, is there anything you would like to ask us?
Mr. Richardson:	Yeah. What are you guys doing?
Tarzan:	Well, Jane and I live in the jungle and I beat up lions.
Mr. Richardson:	Why?
Tarzan:	Because Jane keeps running through the jungle and tripping on branches right in front of them.

Jane:	I do not.
Tarzan:	You do, too.
Mr. Richardson:	What's your monkey's name?
Tarzan:	Do you mean Jane?
Mr. Richardson:	No, the other monkey.

We all cracked up at that one. Mrs. Larson must have been listening from the other room because she laughed at the same time we did.

Jane:	Tarzan, who designs your clothes?
Tarzan:	Jane, see that two-ton elephant over there? If I say "oon-gawa" just once, within two seconds he'll be sitting on your head.
Mr. Richardson:	What do you eat here in the jungle?
Jane:	Snakes, lion meat, bugs, and crocodile brains.
Tarzan:	Yeah, and that's just for dessert.

The three of us were sure we were the funniest thing to ever hit Stillwater. We told the same jokes over and over until they weren't funny anymore. After a while we quit and watched Tarzan climb trees. Then we turned the sound back up. Angry men had found Tarzan's family in a treehouse and were trying to climb a ladder to get them. Then it hit me that Tommy could get up and down to our cave if we used ladders. Sandy agreed, but Tommy wasn't too sure.

"A ladder could tip over or I could fall off it."

"Do you think that could happen?" I asked Sandy. She nodded.

We watched the show again as Tarzan threw some men out of the treehouse to the ground below. Tommy tensed as the men hit the ground. "Ouch," he said.

"Maybe," Sandy said, "we could somehow anchor or tie the top of the ladder to the hill so it couldn't tip over. That would work."

"Yeah," I said. "We could pound some stakes into the ground and tie the ladder to them with ropes or wires." Tommy was sitting and watching us uneasily, probably because he was the one who had to take the chances. After more discussion, we agreed it was worth a try.

The rain kept the afternoon drab, and we passed it playing cards and Monopoly. Around five o'clock, Sandy and Tommy had to help get supper ready, so I headed home.

Dad and I walked into the kitchen the next morning just as Mom ran out the door in her sneakers. "Dad, what's wrong? Why's Mom running?"

"She's starting to jog today. She wants to get in better shape. Her birthday is coming up soon. She always begins to exercise right before her birthday."

"So, what are you up to today, Matthew—that is, after you mow the lawn?"

"Again?"

"Yes, it's been two weeks. A guy with a trailer full of sheep made me an offer last night, but I told him my son needs something to do this summer. I just couldn't deprive you."

"I get the message, Dad. Getting back to your question, I'm gonna build something today and I need some wood. Could I have the two-by-fours in the garage?"

"I guess so. What are you going to build?"

"Oh, I think, ah, well, a ladder."

"A ladder? What do you need a ladder for?"

"Well, you never know, Dad. I might have to climb somewhere. You know, to get cats out of trees, balls out of rain gutters, kites out of trees, or I might have to climb a cliff or something like that."

"Okay, okay," Dad said cutting me off. "You can have the wood, and I think there's a cardboard box in the garage someplace with some nails in it." Dad leaned back and sipped his coffee. "I don't have any long boards in there, Matthew, but I just remembered that they're tearing down that old hotel downtown."

"Yeah?"

"Maybe you and your friends could salvage some long boards. You could ask the workers if you could have some old boards, but don't get in the way."

"Hey, good idea, Dad. Tommy's got a big three-wheel bike and we could haul them back on that."

"Sounds good. Better take gloves along. Slivers, you know. By the way, before I forget, I want you to start hitting the reading a little, like Ms. Schmidke said. She told you to keep reading so you won't lose all the good work you did last year."

Something inside me groaned, but I knew not to groan out loud. "Dad, do I have to? I just hate reading. I had such a neat day planned and reading is so boring."

"You mean it's hard," Dad said, carrying his dishes to the sink. "You need to spend fifteen minutes a day with a book—reading it—not just looking at the pictures."

"All right," I said weakly.

"Matthew, it's not that difficult. You act like I just asked you to work in a coal mine or something. If you're going to improve your reading, you've got to do your part. Ms. Schmidke can't read for you."

"Okay Dad, I'll do it, but I'm not looking forward to it. I don't see what's so important about reading, anyway."

"We've been through this before, Matthew. You don't want to hear my lecture on why it's important to read again, do you?"

"No thanks. I guess I've got it down pretty good by now."

"Since you're going to be downtown anyway, why don't you stop at the library for a few minutes and find something you're interested in, like outdoor survival, camping, or how about a book on astronomy? You and Tommy and Sandy are always talking about astronomy. Stop in and take a look."

"How about if I start on Monday?"

"Today," he said in a low, unfunny voice that meant business.

Before I could turn around, Mom came bursting in the front door. I thought she had forgotten something because she was back so soon. She leaned forward like she was going to throw up. She was breathing really hard. Then she staggered across the kitchen floor. "Quick, get me to the couch," she said between gasps.

"Are you all right, Margaret?" Dad asked.

Mom staggered to the couch, turned, and fell on her back. Dad repeated, "Are you all right, honey?"

"Just . . . give me a few minutes . . . a whirlpool . . . and an oxygen tent. I'll be fine."

"How far did you go?" I asked.

"It's not how far you go. . . . It's how much pain you inflict on your out-of-shape body that counts."

"Mom," I said, "you were only gone five minutes." She didn't answer; she just kept breathing.

"Margaret," Dad said with a grin, "do you want me to call the paramedics?"

Mom looked at him and breathed hard. "No, dear, I don't think so, but you might want to keep the number of the priest handy."

"You know, Margaret, you're supposed to work up to your distance, not go out and kill yourself the first day."

"Listen, dear, if I went any less distance, I wouldn't have gotten over our property line. Oh, by the way, if worse comes to worse, don't call the priest. I wouldn't want him to see me like this." Dad was cracking up.

"Martin dear, there is one more thing I want to say before I go. I want you to remarry, but not to anyone taller or better looking than I am."

"Or in better shape," Dad commented.

"Very funny," Mom added. "I'm taking my last breath and your father is making light of it. Martin, one more request. On my tombstone, I want you to write: She died improving her health — for her family."

"Margaret," Dad said, getting his briefcase, "you're a wonderful person."

"Yes," Mom said, "I was, wasn't I?"

Sandy, Tommy, and I had a busy day. I mowed the grass when it was still wet. The clods of grass gummed up the mower so it died seven times.

When the mowing was done, the three of us rode our bikes downtown to the library and then to the old hotel, or what was left of it. A lot of the boards were stacked in neat piles near the sidewalk. We asked an older man with a silver work hat and a leathery face if we could have four boards. He looked around once to see if anyone was looking and said, "Yeah, go ahead, but don't leave 'em laying around in the street or you know who'll catch it."

We thanked him about a million times, pulled on our gloves, and began to load Tommy's three-wheeler. The boards were sixteen feet long, two inches thick, and six inches wide. In other words, they were heavy. Tommy's poor bike practically groaned. We balanced the boards between the front handle bars and the big basket in the back. The tires were squashed down so the rims were right down on the pavement.

We decided we'd better make two trips. That meant two trips up that huge, winding hill — on foot.

We reminded Tommy more than once that the ladders were for him. As the day grew hotter, the hill grew steeper. All the boards were finally dumped on my driveway with a heavy, clunking sound. Sandy and I plopped down exhausted between the clods of grass on the shady side of the house, and Tommy ran off toward his house. He was back in what seemed like seconds with a saw and hammer.

"Tommy," I said tiredly, "you're making me hot." He didn't seem to get hot or tired ever. It was like no one ever told him he should be tired, so he never got that way.

"Come and sit down, Tommy. I think we've got to do a little planning. You know, we can't go rushing into this building stuff, at least until we mooch something to drink off my mom." Mom wasn't in the mood to be bothered, so we had to drink from the vinyl hose that made the water smell like nail-polish remover.

We never really did plan how to build those ladders. We made the rungs from the wood my dad gave us. We cut them about the length a ladder step should be. We sawed and hammered, and sawed and hammered some more. It took us about three hours for the first ladder, and almost two hours for the second one. The second one didn't look much better than the first, except it didn't have as many bent nails.

One thing we hadn't thought of was how we would move the ladders after we got them built. The three of us couldn't lift either ladder. Instead, we dragged the ladders, one at a time, across the back-yard. It looked like a train had driven across the grass. We continued into the weeds, down the slope, and out to the edge of the bluff. It was work, hard work. Sandy and I were huffing and sweating. Tommy didn't seem to be working up much of a sweat, so I began to watch him. He didn't seem to be doing his share of the pulling. I didn't say anything, but I was think-ing, "We're going through all this work for you, and you're hardly doing anything!"

It took us about half an hour to move that lad-der. Part of the problem was that whenever Sandy and I heaved, Tommy seemed to ho, and whenever we hoed, he heaved. I kept getting madder, but I didn't say anything. We finally dragged the ladder up to the edge of the bluff.

"We did it!" Tommy said, smiling at me. I looked away and kept my mouth shut.

"Let's get this thing over the edge. It's getting late," I said in a mean voice. I started sliding it slowly toward the edge and the weight got to be too much. It started to drop like the end of a teeter-totter with only one kid on it. Our end swung up pretty fast, so Sandy and I let go, but Tommy held on. Suddenly he was up in the air three feet kicking his legs. Sandy, thinking quickly once again, pulled him off just as the ladder slid down the cliff, bounced twice, and dropped flat on the ground below.

All my anger at Tommy came out at once. I let loose with a word my dad uses whenever he bangs his knuckles. Tommy looked at me and grinned. "You said a bad word."

"Oh, shut up!" I said meanly. "So what?" I gritted my teeth and narrowed my eyes at him. "Listen, if it wasn't for you, we wouldn't even have to make this stupid thing. You could at least help! I've got three slivers in my hand and about twenty bruises on my shins because you can't walk straight."

Sandy stuck up for Tommy like she always did. "Shut up, Matthew!" She brought her face right up to mine. "Leave him alone. He's doing the best he can. Just because you're Mr. Perfect doesn't mean you can pick on my brother."

Tommy didn't show anything on his face while Sandy and I argued about him. He pretty much stood and watched as Sandy and I yelled back and forth, saying things I didn't really remember later.

Sandy and Tommy left right after Sandy called me a "brat." That was right after I called her a "dumb girl." As they walked away, I asked myself why I was hanging around with a girl. Back in St. Paul, there were plenty of guys to hang around with. We sometimes had crushes on girls, but we'd never be caught dead hanging around with girls like they were regular friends. We just didn't do it. Now here I was in Stillwater, and the only kids around were a dumb tomboy and her even dumber brother.

I went down to the cave for a while, thinking it would make me feel better. It didn't. I felt awful. I kept thinking of all the great insults I could throw at Sandy the next time I saw her. I felt like screaming, punching, throwing up, and going to sleep, all at the same time. The cave just seemed quiet and empty. I decided to go home.

I discovered Mom had survived exercising, but she wasn't home. At suppertime, Dad and I found a box of macaroni and cheese on the counter with a note from Mom. It read: "Shopping for exercise bike. If you two want to get fancy, there's a can of lima beans in the cupboard above the blender. See you later. I love you both. Mom."

Dad ruined the macaroni and cheese. And the lima beans were dry. Dad reminded me of my reading. The electricity was knocked out and I had no friends. The night didn't cool off like it usually does. The breeze died down and the air got sticky. There was no cool spot on my pillowcase. I went to sleep hoping my dreams would be good.

Chapter 12

The next morning the sky was clear and light blue. A cool breeze punched my bedroom curtains like sheets hanging on a clothesline. I got up. I poured myself a bowl of cereal. Same old Cheerios, same old two-percent milk, same old teaspoon of sugar, same old Tupperware cup of orange juice. I've noticed that sleeping doesn't solve problems. I always feel just as lousy when I wake up as when I went to sleep.

I finished my juice and walked over to the sink to dump my dirty dishes. "Say, Mom, I don't have much to do today. Um, do you have any work to do around here, like the dishes or the wash or something?"

"Did you have a fight with your friends or something?" she asked.

"Mom," I said, flopping down on a chair, "did you go to Mom's Mind Reading School or something? How'd you know? Did you talk to Sandy or Tommy this morning?" Mom smiled and shook her head. "I know, you talked to Mrs. Larson. Right?"

"No, neither. Let's just call it mother's instinct. If I told you all my secrets, half of the fun of being a parent would be gone. So, what happened with your friends?"

"Oh, I don't know," I said, "I think I need some new friends. Tommy drives me crazy, and I don't know about hanging around with a girl."

"As far as I can see, Tommy does just about as well as he can. You can't expect him to keep up with you like your old friends in St. Paul. I think it's wonderful the way you've included him in everything. His mother was telling me that he really doesn't have any friends to speak of. You've been very good for him."

"But, Mom, it's just not that much fun for me. He doesn't get my jokes. He can hardly catch. I'm afraid he's going to break his nose or something. He always interrupts. And those questions! I don't believe I keep answering them!"

"Matthew, nobody expects Tommy to be your best friend. You may be his best friend, but I guess that's just because you've been willing to spend some time with him. Don't worry, you'll be making new friends at school in a couple months. It hasn't been that awful, has it? You seem to be having a good time whenever I see you."

I thought about it for a while. "I guess you're right, Mom. I feel kind of bad. I lost my temper with Tommy yesterday and really yelled at him. Then I started in at Sandy, too. She was just trying to stick up for her brother. I just don't know about this having a girl for a friend. Maybe I can just keep busy around here until the summer is over and football starts."

"I really don't see anything wrong with having a girl as a friend, Matthew. I thought maybe you were a little sweet on her."

"Oh, Mom!" I said with a look of pain on my face. "That's not true. She's just like a boy. You know, she's strong, and tough, and smart, that's all!"

"And cute," Mom added.

"I s'pose she's cute, but she can do all the stuff the guys can do. That's why I like her, or why I used to like her. She's a tomboy. You know, she's kind of like a boy."

"Oh, I see," Mom said, smiling as if she knew something different. "Are you going to make up with them? It'd be a shame to lose a couple of nice friends like that."

"I don't know. I was thinking if I waited long enough they would come over here and apologize to me. Then I'd think about it for a while and let them suffer a little."

Mom said Uh-huh and wiped some crumbs from the counter. "Matthew, do you know what your dad and I do when we've gotten into an argument?"

"No, what?"

"It took us a long time to learn this, but now each of us tells his or her side of things without interruption. The other one has to listen. When each of us has had a turn, we compromise. We work out a deal that we each think is fair so we won't get into the same argument again."

"What does that do? How do you know who wins?"

"What it does is, it makes both of us listen to the other person's point of view. Most of the time, as it turns out, one of us misunderstood the other, or one of us was tired or grouchy."

"I already know both sides of the story, Mom. I'm right and they're brats."

"I'm sure you don't mean that. Just think about it and let me know how it works." Mom opened up the back door and looked out. "I don't see Tommy and Sandy coming over here on their hands and knees, Matthew. I think you better do something. Or I can make long lists of jobs to do around the house for the rest of the summer, if that's what you really want."

After dressing, I walked out in the backyard and looked up the hill to see if Tommy and Sandy were out. I didn't see anybody. I walked along the driveway where we had made the ladders yesterday. There were puddles of water from washing the car the night before. The sun was heating up the blacktop and causing the shallow puddles of water to turn to steam. There, lying in one of the puddles, was Tommy's hammer all covered with rust. I wiped it down with an oily rag from the garage and carried it to Tommy and Sandy's house. I was feeling more nervous than when I was on stage at Pioneer Park.

Aluminum screen doors rattle so loudly when they're knocked on that it drives me crazy. Mrs. Larson answered the door cheerfully. "Good morning, Matthew. Come on in. The kids are doing the morning dishes." As I stepped into the kitchen, the aluminum door slammed shut behind me. Tommy didn't look up, but Sandy did.

"Hi," she said weakly, without smiling. Tommy's Hi was the same as always.

They kept working on the dishes, clinking the glasses and rattling the silverware on the bottom of the sink. Then Tommy began looking back and forth from Sandy, to me, to his mom. No one said anything. I stood by the door, feeling stupid.

Mrs. Larson finally said, "My, you kids aren't too talkative this morning, are you?" No one said anything. She shrugged her shoulders and went into the yard. Tommy finally noticed the hammer.

"There's my hammer. Where did you find it?"

"Oh yeah, I found it in a puddle in our driveway. It was pretty rusty, so I cleaned it off and wiped it down with an oily rag. That'll keep it from getting rusty again." Sandy kept doing the dishes.

"Tommy," Sandy said softly, without looking up, "you should thank Matthew for bringing your hammer back."

"Thank you," Tommy said automatically.

"That's okay," I said. "Really, I didn't mind." Sandy still seemed pretty mad. Tommy didn't seem too upset about anything, and I wasn't really mad anymore.

"I think it would be a good idea if we all had a talk." I had said it, but I didn't really know what to do next. Tommy waited. Sandy finally turned away from the sink and listened. "You see, everybody takes a turn telling his side of why they were mad, and everybody listens 'til they're done. Okay, who wants to go first?" Tommy didn't seem to get what I was trying to say at first and Sandy, if she knew, wasn't letting on. "Okay," I said, "if you want me to go first, I guess I can."

"I think I was mad yesterday because I was tired and grouchy. When I was little and got crabby I was put down for a nap. Maybe, I just needed a nap. I also got mad because Tommy, well . . . you do things slower than I'm used to. I'm just not used to having to watch out for anybody except me. I never had a little brother. That ladder falling was the final thing. I shouldn't have talked so mean. Sorry, Tommy. And I guess I didn't need to get so mad at you either, Sandy. Maybe, next time we shouldn't try to do so much in one day."

Sandy cut in. "I don't like anybody yelling at my brother. I've been watching over him ever since we were little kids. You see, he just doesn't talk fast enough. He can't argue very well, and he can't fight back. I hate it when kids are mean to him just because he won't fight back. So, next time you get grouchy or whatever, just lay off my brother."

I kept my mouth shut even though I felt like arguing. I felt like saying that Tommy had it coming, that he deserved to be yelled at, but I knew Sandy was right. If it had been Robert back in St. Paul, I wouldn't have yelled so much. But I knew that Tommy wouldn't fight back.

Tommy had been taking in what Sandy was saying. He didn't like it. "Sandy, I can take care of myself. I'm not a baby."

"I know you're not a baby, Tommy. I'm just used to helping out." Sandy rinsed off her hands.

"I'm not a baby," he repeated. Tommy reached for the sprayer to rinse the soap off the dishes. He accidentally squeezed the sprayer handle and pointed it toward Sandy just as she turned the faucet on full force. In an instant Sandy was drenched. Her mouth and eyes sprung open in surprise.

"Tommy, I'm going to strangle you!" Tommy's mouth and eyes were wide open, too. Before he could do anything, Sandy grabbed the sprayer from him. Tommy looked at Sandy's wet clothes and said, laughing, "Sandy, it looks like you wet your pants."

Sandy looked down at herself and began to laugh. Tommy was laughing and hopping back and forth. Then Sandy surprised us both by wrapping her hands around the sprayer and shooting water all over Tommy's pants.

"Don't pick on your brother," I said. "Remember what you told me." Things were starting to get a little wild so that probably wasn't the smartest thing to say. Sandy spun around and shot water at me. I dodged left just as Mrs. Larson opened the door behind me. Now all the Larsons were wet. Mrs. Larson had the same look on her face as Sandy did. It must run in the family.

The three of us each got a scolding and a towel. Even though Mrs. Larson was pretty mad, we had a hard time not laughing out loud. It was very much like laughing in church when you're not supposed to. Everything seems ten times funnier than usual.

After we had dried the kitchen and Sandy and Tommy had put on dry clothes, the three of us set out to finish our ladder project. We dragged the second ladder to the hill. We stood the first ladder up and anchored it down with rope and a couple stakes we had made by chopping the ends off two-by-fours. We took turns driving the stakes into the ground with a maul. Tommy had to cut his turn short because he almost hit himself on the foot two times.

Sandy and I were so pleased with the ladder that we went up and down the thing about five times. Then the two of us piled leaves and grasses and soft twigs all around the base of the ladder. If Tommy fell, he would fall into the pile and not break anything. Tommy watched as best he could, making sure he stayed a safe distance from the ledge. When we were finished, we called up to Tommy.

"Hey, Tommy, it's all done. There's a soft pile of stuff in case you fall. Come on down." Tommy didn't say anything.

"What's wrong now?" I asked.

"I might fall," he answered. I groaned and fell into the pile of leaves.

"You know," Sandy said to me, "he could fall from anywhere on the ladder. I never thought of that, either. If he fell from the top, I don't think that pile would be enough."

"Well, then, how are we going to get him down here? With a parachute?" I asked.

"No," Sandy laughed, "we don't have one, and I don't think it would open in time anyway."

"How about a mountain-climber's rope? How do those work?"

"I don't know," Sandy answered. "What else could we use?"

"What if we tied him to the ladder?" I said, joking. "Then he couldn't fall off."

"How could he climb down then?" Sandy wanted to know.

"Sandy, I was just kidding."

"You know," she said, "he could untie himself, go down a step and then tie himself up again. It might take a while, but at least he could get down."

"I see two things wrong—Tommy doesn't tie that well, and he'd have to untie himself as soon as he got himself tied up again. It doesn't make sense."

"What if we used two ropes? Then," she went on, "he would always be tied. That's it! He could bring the two ropes down the ladder with him."

I noticed she had forgotten one thing. "Sandy, you forgot that Tommy doesn't tie that well."

"That's right," she agreed. "There must be some other way he can fasten himself to the ladder and work his way down."

A great idea hit me. "I know, what if we use chain and those hooks like they have on dog leashes? He could snap them without any problem."

"I'll bet that would work," she said, nodding. "Now all we have to do is get some chain and hooks."

"That's where I got the idea," I responded, "from dog chains. We've got some dog leashes from our old dog Lucas. I think they're hanging in our garage."

Tommy wasn't too sure about the idea, but he was outvoted, two to one. It struck me, as I was running back to the house, how much smarter I feel during the summer than during the rest of the year. Maybe that's one of the reasons, or maybe that's *the* reason, I don't like reading in the summer. It reminds me of school, where I feel angry about half the time.

Tommy looked kind of strange with two chains wrapped around his waist that hung down to his knees. He looked just like he had escaped from someplace.

He didn't want to try it at first, but with lots of coaxing and promises to go down with him the first couple of times, he agreed. "There's no way you could fall," I promised. He crawled near the ladder and hooked one of the chains onto the top step.

"I might fall," he said again, watching my face.

"How can you fall?" I asked. "You're chained to the ladder, and the ladder is tied to the hill. Besides, we've got you. Just try it."

He slid himself onto the ladder. "I didn't fall," he said smiling. "It works."

"Now the other chain, Tommy," Sandy said. He took the second chain, wrapped it around the second step of the ladder, and hooked it. Then he stepped down another step, unfastened the chain on the first step, went down another step, and fastened the chain onto the third step. Down he went, step by step, chains clinking and clanking as he went.

"I did it!" he yelled up. Sandy whistled, and I whooped and clapped for him. "That was easy. I want to do it again," he said, as he headed for the ladder to come back up.

"No, wait Tommy," Sandy shouted down. "We'll throw the other ladder down so we can all get to the cave today. Move out of the way."

By four o'clock the three of us were all in the cave. We knew we were pretty clever and felt like we were the masters of the St. Croix Valley.

Chapter 13

After we had chopped off a few branches from the tree in front of the entrance, our cave made a wonderful lookout point. Sandy called it "pruning" and said it wouldn't hurt the tree. After a week or so of sitting on the sandy cave floor, we decided that the cave needed some furniture. There were a lot of garage sales during the summer and we got some terrific stuff. I bought a faded, green-and-white-striped folding lawn chair for fifty cents. Some of the nylon straps were missing, so I fell through the back the first couple of times I sat in it. I fixed it with rope tied across the back. Sandy bought a wooden chair for seventy-five cents and a jug for water. For thirty-five cents Tommy bought an old kerosene lantern that didn't have a wick or any kerosene in it. It really did look good in the cave, though. He also got a canvas captain's chair for a dollar. It had a little holder on the side for cans of pop. It had sweat stains on the back but they didn't seem to rub off on anything.

The cave was comfortable and well-furnished. Our parents knew we had a fort somewhere out back with furniture, but they didn't know it was on the side of the cliff.

"There's no use worrying them," I said. "They don't know how safe it is, and we do."

One morning, when we were walking between the ladders, we found what was left of a dead animal. Fur was scattered all over. It was such a mess we couldn't tell what it was, at first.

"Yuck!" said Tommy. "What's that?"

"I think it was a rabbit," I whispered.

We moved quickly along the path and up the ladder to the cave. Once Tommy had all his chains off Sandy asked, "What do you think killed it?"

"Maybe it was a badger," I answered. "Wisconsin's right across the river and it's called the Badger State. Badgers are bad news according to Mr. Wetzel, my teacher last year. They'll take on any animal, no matter how big or tough."

"It might get us," Tommy said, worriedly.

Sandy looked at us as if we were crazy. "How's a badger going to get across the river and find its way up here? You know, it could just be a fox, or an owl, or something like that. I hear owls hooting out here every night. You two are just making something out of nothing."

"I think we should go," Tommy said.

"Sandy," I said, in a spooky voice, "a badger might be coming up here at night and sitting in your chair."

"I think we should go," Tommy said again.

"Yeah," I agreed, "let's leave Sandy up here alone. She's so brave, she won't mind."

"Fine with me," she said, "I'll finally get some peace and quiet. Good-bye."

"Say, Tommy," I said, "let's go over to the Jenkins's house this afternoon. We haven't been there for a while."

"What about me?" Sandy said, "Don't I get invited?"

"Well," I said, "you seemed so anxious to stay here and face the badger that I didn't want you to miss it. Sandy, are you looking for an excuse to get out of here so you don't have to be here alone?"

"No, Matthew, I'm-not-looking-for-an-excuse-to-get-out-of-here-so-I-don't-have-to-be-here-alone," Sandy retorted, sticking out her tongue at me.

"It kind of seems like it," I said, raising my eyebrows.

"Well, you're wrong. Let's go."

Before we left, I took a stick and smoothed out all of our tracks on the cave floor, so if anything came while we were gone we would be able to see the tracks in the morning. Then the three of us hustled away down the path, moving our eyes as quickly as our feet.

The next morning, after our chores were finished, we made our way to the cave to check for tracks. Nobody wanted to lead the way. I pretty much ended up leading, not so much because I wanted to go first, but because I was going the least slowly. We went down the ladder and along the path without seeing a thing.

I slowly went up the ladder to the cave, feeling a little safer now. I peeked over the top step of the ladder.

"Oh, oh," I said softly. My eyes were about as big as silver dollars.

"What's wrong?" Sandy whispered.

"There's some kind of tracks up here, and we didn't make them."

"What do they look like?" Sandy asked.

"I don't know, but whatever it was, it was bigger than a fox or an owl. It looks like it was kind of shuffling around and dragging its feet. Looks like it has some kind of toes or claws."

"I think we should get out of here," I said. "Yesterday we thought there might be some kind of animal here. Today we *know* there's one. Let's go!"

We exploded down the ladder and hit the ground with our feet already running. Tommy was just walking toward the cave because it took him so long on the first ladder with his chains. He saw us running toward him at full speed with wild looks on our faces. We didn't have to tell him to start running. He headed back at a gallop.

We had just about caught up with Tommy when his foot caught on a root. He fell flat, sprawling on the path. He was too close for Sandy and me to veer to the side. In an instant, all three of us were a tangle of arms and legs. As I got to my feet, I saw movement in the bushes. I looked at Sandy and Tommy. They had seen it, too. We practically flew the rest of the way to the ladder. None of us looked back. Tommy went up first and didn't even stop to fasten the chains. He moved pretty fast, even though it seemed like forever. My heart pounded and I felt so strong that I might have been able to climb up the cliff wall, but I waited. Finally all three of us were at the top. I looked back down at the bushes one last time before running home. There was something coming out of the bushes onto the path. I leaned forward for a better look. A girl stepped out of the bushes.

The girl looked a little younger than Sandy or me. She squinted up at us, shielding her eyes from the sun with her hand. The girl had bright-red hair that hung in a long braid down her back. When she looked up, I saw that she had pale brown freckles that ran down both sides of her nose and across her cheekbones. She wore a green-striped T-shirt and white shorts. And she was barefoot. She walked the rest of the way down the path and began climbing the ladder.

"Hi," I yelled down. "Who are you?" She didn't answer. In fact, she acted like she didn't even hear me. "Hey, Sandy, here's our monster," I said, with great relief. Sandy and Tommy came to the ladder and looked down at the girl who was slowly making her way up.

"Isn't she afraid of the badger?" Tommy asked in a frightened voice.

"What badger?" I said. "She is the badger."

"That's not a badger," Tommy said. "That's a girl."

"Never mind, Tommy. I'll explain it to you later."

The girl was nearing the top of the ladder. "Hi," I said. Still no answer. "Yoo hoo," I tried, "you on the ladder, hello." This time she looked up at me. She grinned and waved.

"You really scared us," Sandy exclaimed. "We thought you were a badger or something. That's why we were running. Who are you and how'd you find our cave?"

The girl didn't answer Sandy. She shook her head and pointed to her ear. She said something we didn't understand. At first, I thought she was talking a different language. "Maybe she's speaking Irish or something," I said. "She kind of looks Irish, with her red hair and all." I looked her in the eyes. "Are you speaking Irish or something?" She shook her head quickly. "How about Spanish? *La casa*?" She still shook her head and lowered her eyebrows.

"What did you ask her?" Sandy asked me.

"I think it means 'the house.'"

"Why did you ask her about a house? We're trying to find out her name."

"It's the only word I know in Spanish."

Again the girl shook her head, pointed to her ear, and said something we didn't understand. "You know what?" said Sandy, "I think she's trying to say she can't hear."

"Can't you hear?" Sandy asked her.

"How's she supposed to answer you, Sandy, if she can't hear?" I asked her. To my surprise, the girl shook her head No. How'd she do that? How can she answer if she didn't hear you?"

"I don't know," Sandy said, "Maybe she just guessed."

"You know, I heard some people can read speech," Tommy said. "They told us about it in school."

"That's right," Sandy said. "I'll bet that's why she didn't answer you when she was coming up the ladder."

Sandy shook her hand a little to get the girl to look at her. "What's your name?"

The girl answered something strange sounding. It sounded like "Lah-ah." Her voice really sounded different.

"Lah-ah?" Sandy said, "That can't be right. I never heard that name before."

The girl shook her head and bent down to write in the dirt. "Oh," Sandy said happily, "she spelled Laura. Her name is Laura." The girl smiled and nodded.

"Where do you live?" I asked Laura. Laura signaled us to follow her. She brought us to the edge of the wooded area where the tall grasses grow. We could see our houses. She pointed to a house that was two up the hill from Tommy and Sandy's.

"That's the Berger's house," Sandy said. "They don't have any kids."

"Think she's lying?" I asked, without moving my lips.

"No," Sandy said in a disgusted voice. "Maybe she's visiting or something."

We stood there for a while wondering what to say. Laura signaled to us that she wanted to know our names.

We invited Laura back to the cave on the condition that she promised not to tell anyone where it was. It took a lot of time to get through to her what we were asking, but once she got it, she didn't waste any time promising. Back in the cave, it was a lot easier to get to know Laura. First, she asked us to sit facing the cave opening. She could see our mouths better since the sunlight coming in the cave would be on our faces. Then she got a stick and wrote in the sand. "Staying with aunt and uncle a few weeks. Mom and Dad in Europe on vacation."

I found out that Laura went to a regular school in Bloomington. They have people in the school who help the kids who can't hear. The helpers translate into sign language what the teacher is saying. Other kids in the class take notes in a special notebook that makes a copy at the same time. The kids who don't hear get the extra copy so they don't have to look away from the person signing.

The four of us loafed around for the rest of the morning watching the wind tumble the clouds across the sky. We also watched the speedboats on the river below, buzzing around in big circles like little water bugs. We took turns using Tommy's binocular.

Even though he drives me nuts some of the time, Tommy is really good about lending people his stuff. He doesn't seem to mind. I wondered if he got ripped off a lot at school. I guessed that kids often asked to borrow his books or lunch tickets or money. He probably forgot to ask for his stuff back.

By lunchtime, the four of us were bored and hungry. We walked Laura back to the Berger's house. Mrs. Berger came out, storming mad, as soon as she saw us.

"Laura, where have you been?" she asked sharply. "I've been looking and calling all over town for you. I've been worried sick." Mrs. Berger had been ignoring us and must have noticed suddenly that we were there. "Hello, Sandy and Tommy and . . ."

"Matthew," I finished for her.

"And Matthew," she said, in the same sharp voice.

Laura looked embarrassed. Her face got red and she looked down at the ground. Mrs. Berger walked up to Laura and moved her hair away from her ears.

"And where are your hearing aids?" she asked, like she couldn't believe it.

Laura began signing and talking at the same time. I couldn't understand her. Mrs. Berger understood most of it, judging by the look on her face.

"In the house? Your hearing aids are in the house? Why?"

Laura signed and talked some more. "Your mother said you were to wear those aids unless you were sleeping or taking a bath."

Laura glanced at us every so often. Mrs. Berger was really embarrassing Laura. Little tears welled in the corners of Laura's eyes. The next time she glanced over at us, she fled Mrs. Berger's questions and ran into the house.

"Laura!" Mrs. Berger called after her.

Sandy, Tommy, and I stood side-by-side watching Mrs. Berger as she turned toward us. Sandy spoke up. "Sorry, Mrs. Berger. It was our fault. We met Laura earlier this morning and asked her to stay with us. We didn't know you would be worried about her."

"Well, I'm responsible for her. Laura is an exceptional girl. She's not like other children, you know. My sister asked me to take care of her for a few weeks, and I'd never forgive myself if anything happened to her. You children understand, don't you?"

We all nodded.

"I don't think you have to worry, Mrs. Berger," I said. "We were just talking. We weren't doing anything dangerous."

"Oh, I'm sure you weren't, Matthew. I suppose I got carried away. It's not as though you were scaling cliffs or anything like that." She laughed lightly to herself. The three of us shot guilty glances at each other. "It's just that parenting is new to me. I guess I was a little hard on Laura. What do you kids think?"

Sandy and Tommy didn't say anything, but I nodded and said, "You see, my mom and dad don't yell at me or spank me anymore. They lecture. It takes longer, but it doesn't hurt so much. It leaves me thinking, which is better than leaving me mad or sore. But, when they lecture me, they never do it in front of anybody."

"I suppose I embarrassed her," Mrs. Berger said, looking at the house. "Listen," she went on, rubbing her forehead, "I'd really like it if you children would spend some time with Laura. As I said, she's a special girl and hasn't had the same chances that you've had, so you'll have to remember her limits when you play together."

"Sure," Sandy answered, "you don't have to ask us. We like her. She's nice."

After lunch Sandy, Tommy, and I stopped over to pick up Laura. Laura didn't hear the knock, so Mrs. Berger came to the door. She was in her twenties somewhere, I think. She was on the heavy-set side and had soft, curly hair.

"Hi there," she said, "I'll get Laura for you.

"Laura," she called. There was no answer. "Hang on a second. I keep forgetting that I can't call her."

She disappeared and brought Laura back with her. Laura looked angry with Mrs. Berger when she came to the door. Besides the cold look in her eyes, Laura looked different in another way. Her ponytail was undone and her wild red hair hung from the part in the middle of her head like a big hula skirt.

Laura slipped out the door and waved weakly to Mrs. Berger without looking up.

"Now you children be careful, but have a nice time," Mrs. Berger said as we walked across the back-yard. I felt like saying to Sandy and Tommy that being careful usually means you won't have a good time, but I kept that to myself.

As soon as Mrs. Berger was inside the house, Laura reached up under her hair. When she pulled her hand out, she had a hearing aid in it. Then she pulled a hearing aid out of the other ear and ran into the Berger's garage. She ran back without the aids. She pulled out a big rubber band and put all her hair into a ponytail. She smiled and seemed to walk a lot lighter. Laura signaled for us to follow her as she ran down the path toward the ladder and our cave.

"Why did she put those things in the garage?" Tommy asked. "Don't they work?"

"I don't think she likes the way they look," Sandy said. "I'll bet that's why she had her hair down like that, to cover them up."

We ran after Laura on the path that was forming from all our trips to the ladder. Once in the cave, I asked Laura, "Why did you take your hearing aids off? Don't they work?"

Laura glanced at each of our faces. She pressed her lips together and paused. I think she was trying to decide if we were going to laugh or make fun of her. When she saw we probably weren't, she knelt down in the sand and wrote, "Aids don't help much." She looked at us to see if we understood. I didn't.

"Why did your folks buy them then?"

"Had different hearing aid before. Wouldn't wear it. It helped me hear better, but wouldn't wear it."

"How come?" Tommy asked.

Laura looked down at the sand and smiled a tiny smile. "Ugly," she wrote. She drew a person in the sand. Then right in the middle of the person's chest, she drew a little box. From the box were two wires going to the ears.

"What's that?" Sandy asked. Then, remembering that Laura couldn't hear her, she tapped Laura on the shoulder. Laura turned her head toward Sandy. "What's that?" Sandy repeated.

"Hearing aid," Laura said, pointing at her chest. "Wear it here."

"That's a hearing aid?" Sandy asked. "I thought they went in your ears." As she spoke, Sandy pointed to her ears.

"This one works better." None of us understood what she said. With her finger, she wrote, "Works better." She pointed to the box in the drawing. She continued to write. "Don't wear new aids. Don't help. Sound noisy. Mom mad. Aunt mad."

The three of us watched Laura carefully and nodded. Then she wrote, "Don't like write so much. Teach you fingerspelling? Signs?" She looked up hopefully.

"Yeah!" I exclaimed.

Tommy asked, "What did she say?"

"She wants to teach us to talk with our hands — in signs."

"Like this?" Tommy said, wiggling his fingers and waving his hands.

"Something like that, Tommy," Sandy answered.

Laura didn't waste any time. She smoothed out the sand in front of her and drew the letter "a." She turned around and held her right hand in a loose fist with her thumb up. "A," she said. We each made an "a." She turned and shifted our hands around until she got them just right before she went on to "b."

The letter "b" looks like the way you hold your hand when giving the Boy Scout Pledge. The palm of the hand faces forward with all four fingers straight. The thumb turns in to the middle of the palm. Laura went through the signs for all the letters in the alphabet. Sandy learned the letters quickly and was soon spelling words. I learned the letters pretty quickly, but I don't spell that well, so I mostly watched. Tommy had trouble both learning the letters and spelling. Even so, he learned a couple things and was excited to be able to do them.

Sandy and Laura tried to get me to fingerspell with them. I wanted to be able to talk like Laura so I worked really hard and practiced when I was alone. For some reason it was easier to spell with my hands than with a pencil.

A couple days later Laura fingerspelled that she would show us some signs. Signs, I discovered, don't have any spelling. There are certain ways of moving your hands that mean whole words or ideas. If you want to say "good morning" to someone, instead of spelling it out, you only have to do two things. First, you put your fingertips by your mouth and pull them away. That means "good." Then, with your palm facing you, bend your right arm at the elbow, put your left hand in the bend of the elbow and bring your right hand, toward you. That means "morning."

I must have perked up, because next Laura taught us to sign "'You are happy." For "you" Laura taught us to simply point to the person we were talking to. There is no sign for "is." The word "happy" is made

with the right hand open with the palm in. Fingers point left. Then you pat your chest with little upward movements.

Signing was easier for Tommy, too. So, with all three of us having a better chance to learn, we spent a lot of time at it. In fact, we spent about three or four hours each day. Before long, we were able to sign most things. We felt pretty clever because of our new skill. We got used to Laura's voice, too, and could understand her pretty well.

We went to Alfred and Mertle's house to introduce Laura. Before we left, they learned a few signs. Alfred especially liked the sign for "morning." The last thing we taught them was the sign for "good-bye," which is a side-to-side wave with the right hand, just like I'd always done. The picture in my mind of Alfred will always be him waving good-bye from his porch.

Chapter 14

"Hey, Tommy, who let you out of your cage?" The voice came from the other side of the park where we were having a picnic lunch. Laura, Sandy, Tommy, and I had been to the library to get some books on astronomy. The four of us were finishing our lunches and were about to play cards when the voice interrupted us.

"Looks like Tommy is having a little party," said another voice. Striding across the library park were two boys who looked a year or two older than me. They wore faded, black T-shirts with the sleeves cut off to show their muscles, which weren't all that big. And they wore tight, faded blue jeans and heavy-looking motorcycle boots. They each held a cigarette loosely between their thumb and index finger. They both squinted at us as they sucked smoke through their mouths and blew it out their noses.

The shorter one had straight brown hair that looked like he cut it himself. It came down over his eyes and he had to keep pushing it back so he could see. The taller kid had long curly hair and a thin face. He kept breathing through his mouth. Maybe his nose was plugged up or something.

Sandy had her back to them as they walked up to our picnic table. Her shoulders stiffened and her mouth was shut tight. Sandy stared at a spot on the table and said firmly, "Why don't you guys just keep going and leave us alone?"

"What'd we do?" the shorter one laughingly asked Sandy. "We're just being friendly."

They looked at each other, grinned, and took another drag from their cigarettes. I had seen guys like these in my school in St. Paul. Some of them were really mean, but some were just tough talkers and were pretty nice once I got to know them. I couldn't tell what these guys were really like. I had my own way of handling big talkers. I'm not saying it would work for everybody, but more often than not, if I talk big, too, they don't give me any trouble. It's important not to look scared or bothered. If you do, you won't get rid of them. Tommy timidly watched Sandy and the two guys. He glanced first at me and then at Laura.

"You guys should just get going," Sandy said again. "Why don't you two go for a little swim in the river, and take along a bag of rocks."

The two boys ignored Sandy and walked over to Tommy. "Hey, watcha got here, Tom-Tom? Mmmmm. Chips . . . My favorite . . . Hey, Tommy, can I have a swig of your Coke?" They helped themselves.

"Cut it out!" Sandy ordered through gritted teeth.

The taller kid took another chip and looked right at Sandy as he put it in his mouth. He chewed with his mouth open. His partner flashed a dopey grin and flicked his cigarette. I decided it was my turn to get into the act. One of my problems, according to Dad, is that I sometimes talk first and think later.

"I think you two better pay Tommy for the food you took," I said quietly.

"What?" they laughed.

"You took Tommy's food without asking, and you owe him money," I said, looking them in the eyes. "I'd say about a dollar. He won't want to finish his bottle of pop with your germs all over it, and you finished off his chips. That's about a dollar. There's no such thing as a free lunch." Mr. Wetzel used to tell us that all the time. I don't think it had anything to do with what was happening, but it popped into my head so I said it.

"Well, who's going to collect the money?" the shorter one demanded, sucking on his cigarette. I was afraid of that—they weren't going to back down.

My mouth opened again. "I gotta tell you two that I'm about that far from earning my black belt in Kung-Fu karate." I made a tiny space between my thumb and index finger as I watched them through narrowed eyes.

"Kung what?" the taller one asked.

"Chu Ching's Kung-Fu karate. I've been taking lessons from him since practically before I could walk. At my last school I had to register my hands and feet with the school principal. Really, they're weapons."

"What's your name, kid?"

"Matthew." I thought for a second. "That's my baptized name. My karate name is . . . Bong Fong. . . . It may sound funny, but people don't ever laugh—at least not when I'm around."

"I think you're all talk, Mr. Bong Bong or King Kong, or whatever your name is supposed to be," said the shorter kid.

"No," said the other, "I think it was Ding Dong. Didn't he say it was Ding Dong?"

The only thing I knew about karate was the beginning stance. One day a man had come to school and talked to my class. The only thing he had time to teach us before lunch was the karate stance. My friends and I practiced it and practiced it for a week straight until we could scare each other half to death. We would jump into the stance with a savage "Ahieee-ah!" One fist was at the hip, the other at hip level, but in front a little. Both knees were bent some and the left leg was in front of the right.

I jumped into the stance with the best "Ahieee-ah" and the fiercest look I could manage. I took two quick jabs at an imaginary enemy with what I hoped looked like karate jabs. The boys stepped back a little. They glanced at each other and then watched my feet. I think they were waiting to see if I was going to let them have it. The smart-aleck looks were off their faces now. I wiggled my feet a little to see what they'd do. The taller one took another step back. I tensed my muscles so they were shaking a little. It worked.

The shorter of the two finally smiled and looked at his cigarette. "You know, it's too bad. I was just going to reach into my pocket for a dollar, when I remembered that my money is at home." He shook his head like he was sorry, but his grin said he wasn't.

"You guys think you're so smart, picking on somebody who can't fight back," I said. "Maybe you're tougher than Tommy, but I'll bet he's better than you at a lot of things." My voice started to shake a little. I was scared and mad at the same time. The shaking started in my stomach and worked its way up to my throat. I took a deep breath. They must have noticed, because they got a little bolder.

"Tommy's better than us at a lot of things? Like what?" the shorter one asked, with his eyebrows raised. His partner stepped forward again.

"Yeah, he's better at falling down and spilling his food tray at school."

"Be quiet," Tommy said softly, "or Matthew'll knock your block off." Tommy didn't know I was bluffing.

"Yeah," Sandy said. "You guys better lay off before Matthew flattens you."

I tried to change the subject back to Tommy. "Tommy is good at a lot of things, like, um, ah, remembering stuff. Like, he can remember batting averages, world records, um, what else? Player's numbers, things like that. Tommy, who was the first black pro baseball player?"

"Jackie Robinson, 1947, the Brooklyn Dodgers."

"See?" I said.

"So what?" asked the big talker. "Who cares about that stuff?"

"Well, it's in books," I said smartly. "Somebody must care. Besides, Tommy is also a better card player than you. We were just gonna play a game of poker. Tommy whips us all the time."

"Tommy's a good card player?" The taller one laughed, stretching his head forward like he hadn't heard correctly. "I'll bet he can't even hold the cards right."

"I know," I proposed, "since you owe Tommy money and you're so sure he's a lousy card player, how about if you play a little poker? . . . How about this? Tommy wins, he gets two dollars, you guys win, you get two dollars. Fair enough?"

"Sure," said the big talker, "deal 'em out." He put his cigarette out in the grass and walked toward the table, rubbing his hands together.

"Wait a minute," I said, "we can't play now. You guys don't have your money—do you?"

"Name the place, my man. I love money."

"Okay, one week from today, Wednesday, one o'clock, at my house. It's just a couple houses down from Sandy and Tommy's house. It's green."

All this time, Laura had been watching everything and trying to figure out what was going on. Just as the two guys were about to leave, Laura asked Sandy something in sign language. The thin-faced taller one asked, "What was that?"

"That's sign language," Sandy said snottily. "She's our new friend and that's how she talks. Keep your comments to yourself, if you don't mind."

"This is quite a little group you've got here," said the shorter one, looking right at me. "First, you got Tommy. Then you got a girl who can't talk. Then you got Sandy, a mommy and a tomboy all in one. And then there's Mr. Ding Dong. What's the matter with you?"

"Nothing!" I said angrily. "Just bring your money. Then you won't talk so big!" I felt the blood rushing to my face. "Tommy'll show you!"

The two bullies walked away.

"Tommy's gonna beat your pants off," I shouted after them. They didn't answer me. They lit cigarettes as they headed toward Main Street.

We decided not to play cards just then. Instead, the four of us quietly climbed on our bikes and headed for the marina that Laura's uncle, Mr. Berger, owned. Tommy was lagging behind a little when Sandy rode up beside me.

"Are you crazy? Tommy can't beat Steve and Ed in cards. I sure hope you're the one who's bringing the money."

"Tommy can win," I said, staring ahead. "He just needs practice. We've got a week."

"Practice?" she questioned, looking back over her shoulder. "He'll need a week's practice just to learn how to hold the cards."

"He can win," I said again, without looking up.

"In seven days?" Sandy continued. "Seven weeks, maybe."

"If he really tries, I'll bet he can do it. I don't think he puts his mind to things. We'll help him."

"You know, you're wrong about that. Tommy really does try. He tries twice as hard as any kid I know and still he learns less than half as much. He'll try for you, but I really don't think he can play poker with those guys."

"Well, we'll see."

"Matthew," she continued, "Tommy's the only person I know who doesn't call a club a club, he calls it a clover, a black clover."

"We'll see."

Laura and I took on the job of teaching Tommy. Sandy didn't help because she thought the whole idea was stupid, and she told us so. I quickly learned that Laura was a terrific card player, but it was hard to sign what she knew to Tommy. We weren't doing too well.

I'm a bigger talker than I am a believer. I repeat what I want to happen to convince myself it'll come true. It took two or three days to convince me that Tommy really didn't have a prayer. He truly didn't. Sandy was right. We worked three hours in the mornings and three hours in the afternoons. It wasn't going to be enough.

On the third day, just when I was ready to give up, Steve and Ed paid us a surprise visit. Laura was showing Tommy what beats what in poker, so she didn't see them coming. "Hope your little reject gang has got its moolah collected for the big match on Wednesday," said Steve, the shorter of the two.

"What's moolah?" Tommy asked.

"That's what you're going to lose on Wednesday, Tom-Tom." Steve and Ed laughed in each other's faces.

"What are you guys doing here, anyway?" I asked, with a look on my face like I had just smelled something bad.

"Oh, we wanted to see if your little club will be able to come up with the cash."

"I'm putting up the cash myself," I said, keeping my chin really high. "And I'm not worried about losing it."

"Then you must be awfully rich, kid, or awfully stupid," said Ed, the taller one.

Laura was trying to figure out what was going on. She turned to me and made three signs—one toward her chest, one off her chin, and a finger flick by her forehead. "I don't understand," she signed.

I rubbed the fingertips of my right hand against my thumb to show that Steve and Ed wanted to know about money. I didn't know if it was the sign she used, but she knew what I meant. She rolled her eyes. While Laura and I were signing back and forth, Steve and Ed watched. Out of the corner of my eye, I could see them imitating us. They were making fun of Laura's signing. Laura could see them easily, since my back was to them and she was facing me. She stopped for a moment. Then she signed, "They are tiny blockheads."

I laughed and laughed. Steve and Ed didn't like the idea that we could talk about them, right in front of them, and they could not understand. They figured they were being made fun of, but didn't know how.

"What're you guys talking about?" Steve demanded.

It was fun not telling them. Laura grinned a little victory grin. Suddenly, though, Tommy said, "They said you're both blockheads."

"Tommy!" I moaned. Steve moved toward me with his fist closed. I was just about to try my karate bluff again, when Dad's car pulled into the driveway. Good ol' Dad. Steve stopped and looked around. Dad drove the car down to the garage, which was right near us in the backyard. He got out with his briefcase, looked over, grinned, and said, "Hello, nice day, huh? These two friends of yours, Matthew?"

"Kind of, Dad," I gulped, glancing at Steve and Ed out of the corner of my eye.

"Nice to meet you, boys. Put out those cigarettes, though. We don't allow smoking around here."

"We gotta be going, anyway," Steve said, taking a puff of his cigarette and turning.

"Yeah, gotta go. See you Wednesday," added Ed. With long strides he quickly caught up to Steve.

Dad watched them go and then looked at me as if to say, "Are you sure these two are your friends?" I shrugged my shoulders. Dad shrugged his shoulders and went into the house.

Laura watched Ed and Steve turn the corner of the house and head toward the street. She stared at the spot where they disappeared so long that I finally waved my hand in front of her eyes. She blinked and shook her head as if to say she was okay. Then she lay back in a lawn chair and stared at the tree branches. Laura looked like she was thinking about something, so Tommy and I went back to our card practice.

Tommy worked on shuffling. He knew what he wanted to do. He had his fingers in the right place, but the cards always worked their way out of his hands. It looked like he was holding a handful of watermelon seeds, the way they kept squirting out of his hands.

Several minutes passed before Laura hopped up from the lawn chair and walked to the house. She stood by the den window, looked back toward the table, then walked back to us. She didn't notice us staring at her. Laura looked up into the tree again and then waved us away from the table so she could move it about two feet.

"What's she doing?" Tommy asked.

"Beats me," I said, getting up and looking up into the tree for some kind of clue.

Just then Mrs. Larson called Tommy home for supper. "Tell me later what Laura was doing, Matthew," he said as he backed away. He continued watching Laura so closely that he was about to trip on the edge of the driveway.

"Don't trip on the pavement, Tommy," I called. It was too late. His heel caught and down he went, hard, right on his backside. Tommy got up and, with an embarrassed look, brushed his pants off and hurried away.

"You okay?" I said to him. Tommy didn't turn around or answer.

Laura hadn't been watching us. When I turned back to her I could see her eyes sparkle with great discovery. The sparkle in her eyes quickly spread to a smile. Finally, she looked at me. Laura moved her finger toward her head to sign she had an idea. Then she signed something else. It took a long time for me to understand her, but when at last I figured it out, my reaction was, "That's cheating, Laura!"

She shook her head and made the sign for money. She was saying we wouldn't take the money.

"Wow, that would teach them to watch their big mouths," I said, with some of Laura's sparkle in my smile. Laura read my lips and nodded. Her smile had become sly.

Wednesday arrived. A windless, hot day, the air hung heavily from the clouds like sagging, sweaty clothes. Laura and I made most of the preparations for the big game in the morning. Tommy practiced with Sandy, who was not the most enthusiastic teacher in the world. Sandy wasn't too sure she would even stop by. It was just as well, I thought, since Sandy wouldn't approve of what we were about to do. Sandy is one of those people who is sometimes a little *too* honest. If enemy agents came running up to her door and shouted, "Where are your parents? We need them for questioning," Sandy would probably tell them they were hiding in the basement because she wouldn't want to lie. She would also probably tell Ed and Steve what was up and ruin everything.

Laura had come up with a terrific plan. Tommy had to hold the cards tilted down just enough so Ed and Steve couldn't see them but a video camera sitting up in the tree could. We hung the Berger's video camera from a branch high above the picnic table. We ran the camera cable down the back side of the tree behind some rakes and brooms we leaned there. To get the cable across the grass, we taped it to our garden hose. Then the cable snaked up the wall of the house and in through the den window. Inside, the cable was hooked up to our TV. Laura could see Tommy's cards from the TV set in our den. Then she could sign to Tommy what cards he should or shouldn't play. Tommy would wear clip-on sunglasses over his regular glasses so Ed and Steve couldn't see that Tommy was watching the window. Everything was ready. My Mom had gone shopping for the day in St. Paul, so she wouldn't be home to ask questions. Tommy would hold his cards on a special clipboard we'd rigged up. I had built a little easel for the clipboard to rest against, and turned the clipboard upside down so the clasp was at the bottom. The camera could see the cards in the clasp just fine from its spot above Tommy.

At one o'clock the camera was on, Tommy, wearing his sunglasses, was on his side of the table, and Laura was watching the TV monitor just behind the den window.

"Do you think they're going to come?" Tommy asked nervously.

"Yeah, they'll be here. Ed and Steve think this'll be easy. It's going to be great. Just watch Laura's signs from the window. You can't miss. She plays cards better than any kid I've ever seen."

A few minutes passed. Laura practiced sending Tommy signs. It was one-fifteen when the heavy clomping of boots echoed between our house and the neighbor's. Ed and Steve strode into the backyard like they had already won.

"Hey, Tom-Tom," Steve called, "what's with the shades? You afraid my card playing will be too flashy for you?"

"No, they're for my poker face. Right, Matthew?"

"Yep," I said, glancing toward Laura. She gave me a thumbs-up. Everything was ready.

"Wait," said Steve. "What's with the clipboard?"

"Tommy has a little trouble holding the cards. This keeps them in order." Steve and Ed looked at each other and rolled their eyes.

Ed and Steve sat down across the table, grinning and rubbing their hands together. "This money will be most gratifying, Steven," said Ed.

"My, my, you are most correct, Edward. We must stop by at the Video Arcade afterward and partake in some choice games."

"That would be most satisfactory, Steven."

"Let's begin, gentlemen." Ed leaned forward on his elbows. "I'm ready."

"We'll play five-card draw," I said. "You can open on anything. You can draw up to three cards. You can raise only twice. Blue chips are worth a dime, red chips are worth a nickel, and the white ones are worth a penny. You both have to put in a nickel to be in each game. You each start with two dollars worth of chips and play until one of you is out. Okay?"

"Okay," said Tommy.

"Let's go," Ed said, clapping his hands together. He shuffled the cards and set them out on the table for Tommy to cut. "Cut 'em, Big Tommy." Tommy reached out and lifted half the deck and placed it beside the other half. Ed reached out and, instead of placing the top half on the bottom, he put it back on the top again.

"Wait a minute!" I said. "That's cheating."

Ed pretended he had made a mistake and switched the cards around the right way. Tommy and Ed threw in red chips. Ed gave Steve a sly grin and began to deal the cards. Ed quickly arranged his cards into a perfect fan as Tommy slipped his cards into the clipboard. It was Ed's turn to trade in some cards, and he drew two new ones. Tommy looked past Ed and Steve, toward the window where Laura was sitting. He got the sign, looked back at his cards, and said, "I'll take two."

Tommy pulled the first and third cards out of the clipboard and laid them on the table facedown. Ed looked a little surprised that Tommy understood that much about the game. Ed handed him the cards.

"You ready, Big Tommy?" Tommy looked at the window. He saw Laura give thumbs-up again. "Yes, I'm ready." Tommy threw a red chip on the table, just like Laura signed.

"Okay, I'll see your nickel and raise you a nickel." Ed flipped two red chips into the center of the table and watched Tommy cooly.

"I'll see your nickel and raise you a nickel, too," Tommy shot back.

"I'll see that nickel and raise you another nickel," Ed repeated, and slapped down two more red chips. It seemed to turn into a betting contest. I watched Tommy to make sure he was watching Laura's signs. He was.

"I'll see that and raise you a dime," Tommy said defiantly.

"That's two raises," I said. "Now you have to show your cards."

Tommy had three kings and two fours—a full house. Ed had three queens, an ace, and a jack. Ed groaned and Steve rolled his eyes.

"I won!" Tommy exclaimed. "I beat his pants off, didn't I, Matthew?"

"Yep, you're off to a good start. Hang in there."

"Yeah, just cool it, Big Tommy," said Steve, squinting his eyes. "There's a little luck in this game and that was only the first hand, for Pete's sake. Right, Ed?"

"Yeah, it sure looks that way. Your deal."

I shuffled the cards for Tommy, but he dealt them. It took Tommy about five minutes to deal the cards. That made Ed and Steve pretty edgy.

They played on. For every five games, Tommy won four. The chips piled up on Tommy's side of the table. Ed and Steve bickered with each other. Steve kept telling Ed what to do and Ed kept telling Steve to shut up. Tommy kept reminding Ed and Steve that they were getting their pants beat off.

Every time Tommy won a hand the two of us shouted. Tommy got so excited he bounced up and down. A couple of times I thought he was going to fall off the bench. Finally, Tommy's clip-on sunglasses slipped off and bounced from the table onto the grass. In his haste to find them, Tommy stepped on them. There was a sharp, snapping sound. The piece that held the two lenses together had broken. Tommy would have to play without them. Now, Ed and Steve could see where Tommy was looking.

The next time the cards were dealt, Tommy looked to the window for the signs. After a while Ed said, "Where do you keep looking?" I held my breath. Just as Ed looked around, Laura ducked behind the curtain. "He keeps looking at the house,'" Ed said, looking at me.

"It's ah, well, it's his glasses," I said. "See how thick they are? They make his eyes look faraway. So sometimes you can't really tell where he's looking."

"Well, it sure looks like he's watching the house for something," Ed said suspiciously.

"I know," I said, "that's the way it looked to me, too. I got used to it."

Tommy won that hand even without the sunglasses. Ed shook his head while Steve muttered something to himself. Tommy and I shouted and clapped. The noise must have finally made Sandy curious. She strolled over.

I swallowed hard as she approached the table. Sandy knew Tommy better than anyone, except his mom and dad, so she was sure to figure out what was going on.

I didn't look up. "Tommy, did you win that?" she asked, like she couldn't believe her eyes.

"I'm beating Ed's pants off, even without my sunglasses."

"What are you doing, cheating?" she asked, with a little chuckle.

"Ha. Ha. Ha," I laughed nervously. "That's a good one, Sandy."

"Well, it's hard to believe. I could see Laura winning like this, but, no offense Tommy, I didn't think you could do it." I nodded in agreement.

"By the way," Sandy went on, "have you two seen Laura?"

"Yeah, she's watching TV," I said, grinning sheepishly.

Sandy replied, "No, she's not home. I was just there."

"Oh, um, that's right. She's watching TV at my house."

"Good," said Sandy. "I'll join her. It's got to be a lot more fun than watching some guys play cards."

"Oh," I muttered, "I think it'll be about the same."

Sandy disappeared into the house as Tommy slowly dealt the last hand. Through the window, I could see Sandy sit down on the couch to watch TV. Suddenly, she jumped and leaned forward for a closer look at the TV. Then Sandy looked out the window at us. I shrugged my shoulders and tried to smile. It didn't work. We hadn't told Sandy about our plan because she wouldn't have gone along with it. Now she had walked right into it. I was afraid of what she might do.

Laura was signing like crazy, trying to keep Sandy from blowing everything. Laura couldn't convince Sandy and, lickety-split, Sandy came out of the house. I thought she was headed for the picnic table to tell everything. Instead, Sandy strutted back into the house and a second later appeared in the den window with the unplugged end of an electrical cord in her hand. She held it up and shook it at us. She looked like a mother shaking her finger at naughty kids.

Tommy finished arranging his cards on the clipboard and looked to the window for Laura. She threw up her hands. Tommy looked at me. I shook my head.

Tommy was on his own, and he knew it.

"Just play, Tommy!" Ed demanded impatiently.

Smiling, Sandy walked up to watch us squirm.

"I'm in," Tommy said quiety, and threw in his red chip. Once more he looked toward the window. Laura shook her head.

If only Tommy could win this hand, he would have won the bet and the game would be over. If Ed won, he would have time to catch up, and he would.

"Hit me twice," growled Ed. Tommy gave Ed two cards for the two he had laid down.

"Hit me twice," growled Tommy, just as Ed had.

"You're dealing, ace," Ed told Tommy. He looked at Steve and sighed. He looked back at Tommy. "You have to hit yourself. I'm not dealing. You are. Hit yourself."

Tommy grinned. "That sounds dumb, doesn't it, Sandy? Don't you know you're not supposed to hit yourself?" Tommy was the only one laughing. Ed gritted his teeth. Tommy gave himself two cards and said, "Ouch! I hit myself." I had to hold back a laugh that time.

"Okay," said Ed, "I'll bet five cents." He slid a chip to the middle of the table. Ed still had two red chips left.

It was Tommy's turn. "I'll see your nickel and raise you a nickel." Tommy was on his own and looking good. Ed watched Tommy for some sign of what he might have in his hand. He got more than he hoped for. Tommy looked at me and said in a loud whisper that Ed and Steve could hear, "Matthew, is it good to have two fours?" I closed my eyes. That, of course, is not a good hand. I knew it. Sandy knew it, and for sure, Ed and Steve knew it. Steve laughed loudly and Ed grinned widely.

Tommy answered his own question. "No, that's not good." He was always doing that—asking questions he knew the answer to. This time, it looked like it might cost him the game.

Ed reached for his last two chips. "I'll see your nickel and raise you a nickel." He slid the chips slowly forward and gave Steve a nudge with his elbow. All the while, he kept his eyes on Tommy.

"I'll see your nickel and I'll raise you a nickel," said Tommy. That bet didn't make sense, either.

"Well, I'm out of chips," said Ed. "Let's show 'em." Ed smiled and laid down his hand—three tens, a queen, and a four. It looked like Tommy couldn't beat three of a kind.

Tommy laid down his cards. There was silence. Everybody blinked. Tommy had three aces, a five, and a jack. Surprised, Steve stood up so fast he knocked Ed and the picnic bench over.

"I win," Tommy said loudly. "Right?"

I slapped Tommy on the back while he jumped up and down. Sandy looked coldly at us. Laura came out of the house and gave Tommy a big hug.

Ed got himself up off the ground. "I was tricked! You never had two fours."

"Yes, I did," said Tommy. "I put them down and I got two aces." Tommy had been checking with me to see if they were good cards to get rid of. It was a great joke because Ed and Steve thought Tommy was so bad at cards that he would tell what was in his hand.

Ed and Steve were stunned. Ed slowly reached into his pocket for two dollars. He threw the money on the table and got up to leave.

Sandy cleared her throat. "Say, Ed and Steve, I think there's something you guys should know about." My eyes got as big as poker chips.

I cut Sandy off. "Ah, what she means to say is that our parents, ah, well, really don't let us play for money. So, let's see. How about if we keep a dollar just for Tommy's food. You two can keep the rest. We don't want it." Sandy didn't say anything.

"Naw, you won it," Ed said. "I don't believe it, but you won it fair and square."

Sandy started to open her mouth. Again, I cut her off. "Tell you what. Since we can't keep the money and you don't want it back, how about if we treat for ice cream tomorrow afternoon?"

Ed and Steve looked at each other and shrugged their shoulders. "Yeah, I s'pose so," Ed said.

"Great," I replied. "One o'clock then. We'll see you tomorrow." Ed and Steve walked off slowly. Steve kept shaking his head.

Tommy, Laura, and I treated Ed and Steve to ice cream the next day. Sandy wouldn't come. She still didn't want to have anything to do with the card game. Ed and Steve didn't say much at the dairy bar, and left right after they finished their ice cream. They didn't say Thanks, but they didn't once call Tommy "Tom-Tom," either.

Chapter 15

That first week in August went by as slowly as the houseboats that wandered aimlessly up and down the river. The air hung heavily in the valley. People moved sleepily and as little as possible under its weight. It was work just to breathe. The four of us mostly sat in the cave entrance out of the heat. We spent a good part of the rest of the summer looking out over the river valley. We watched the boats going under the Stillwater bridge, and the cars and trucks going over it. The three of us tried to guess how long the water-skiers would last before falling. Tommy kept a record in a little notebook that never seemed to run out of pages. The boats and skiers looked like they were moving in slow motion. On really hot days things didn't seem to move at all.

The woods had its own smells in August. There was a musty smell of weeds and rotting leaves. There was a spicy-smelling weed I especially liked because it reminded me of the smooth dirt path I walked barefoot to the lake on our vacations up north.

Sometimes, when a breeze drifted up from below the bluff, we got backyard smells—freshly cut, wet grass (the kind that sticks in clumps on the underside of lawnmowers), the smell of barbeque coals and lighter fluid, and occasional whiffs of rosebushes.

We learned some more signs from Laura, answered more of Tommy's questions than we should have, and relived our summer adventures. I told Sandy and Tommy and Laura about Mr. Wetzel. He had moved to Alaska the day after school was out. I had found out from my old friend Robert that his adventures were cut short. A bear did him in. It chased him up a tree and Mr. Wetzel was up there so long he fell asleep. He rolled over and fell about fifteen feet. The noise scared the bear off, but Mr. Wetzel broke his pelvis and had to be flown back to St. Paul. He spent the rest of the summer in a body cast watching soap operas and reruns of "Wild Kingdom."

One Friday afternoon was especially drab. In the late afternoon when the cars from St. Paul became heavy on Highway 95 south of town, we knew it was getting near suppertime. We said nothing as we walked single file back to our yards. It felt like we had said everything there was to say in July.

As we came around the corner of the garage, we saw a delivery truck stop at my house. A man in a brown uniform carried a heavy-looking package to the front door. A delivery truck is a big deal, especially if it stops at your house, and even more especially if it happens on a boring day. The four of us ran quickly to the front of the house. Mom had a puzzled look on her face as she signed for the package.

"Matthew," she said, "this package is for you." It was a box about the size and shape of a golf bag.

"For me?" Mom lowered her eyebrows. "I didn't order anything. Honest, Mom."

I think Mom was worried because once, when I was about eight years old, I ordered a four-hundred dollar cowboy saddle from a mail order catalog. I had charged it. My parents were not happy about that. I didn't know you had to pay the store later when you charged something. I ordered it because I thought if I couldn't have a pony in the city, at least I could have a saddle. They made me send the saddle back. I cried all night. Mom and Dad tried to make me feel better by buying me a toy horse and saddle that sat on the top of my dresser. I hated that horse. After that I stopped dreaming about riding horses.

"What is it?" Laura signed, sliding her index finger down across her left palm. I shook my head—I didn't know.

Tommy asked about ten questions before I got the box open. Looking into the box, I was surprised to see my eyes reflecting off a piece of round glass. I pulled out crumpled newspaper and slid out a telescope.

"That's just like Alfred and Mertle's telescope," Sandy said.

"This *is* their telescope," I said. "See? It's been used. There are some scratches on the paint."

"Look for a note," Mom said. "Maybe that will explain things."

A few taps on the overturned box produced a small envelope. The note said, "Thought you children might enjoy this as much as we have. Your friend, Mrs. Jenkins."

"All right! A telescope!" I shouted. "This is a great day after all."

"Wait a minute," Sandy said. "Why would they give us their telescope? They're really nice and all, but they enjoyed it so much themselves. It's hard to believe they suddenly got sick of it."

"Maybe they got a new one," I said.

"Mr. Jenkins was trying to pay for this one by charging kids to look through it. Remember?"

"Yeah," I said, wrinkling my nose. "It doesn't make sense, does it?"

We decided to bike over to the Jenkins's house. Laura couldn't come because Mrs. Berger didn't think Laura should be "riding on those busy streets." It was true, Laura didn't have experience riding on Stillwater's steep hills. Laura was furious. Her eyes burned like laser beams at Mrs. Berger while she told me why Laura couldn't go.

Sandy and I were puffing and weak-legged by the time we got to the Jenkins's house. Tommy walked his bike up the hill. We snapped down our kickstands and climbed up the steep steps to their house. Halfway up, we stopped suddenly. In the yard was a bright red For Sale sign. And there was a smaller red sign hanging below it that said Sold.

The door was locked. The porch furniture was gone. We looked through the window to the big living room. There was nothing there. The stuffed chairs, the TV in the fireplace, the pictures of all the people in uniform, all gone.

"I don't get it, Sandy. They never said anything about moving. Maybe they just got sick of keeping up this big old house."

"Or maybe they just got sick," Sandy said softly.

I pretended not to hear Sandy. "Let's go ask the next-door neighbors. They should know what's happened." We went next door. We clomped up the wooden steps and knocked. I could hear the clinking of forks and knives as a heavy woman opened the door. She had one of those faces that always seem to be laughing. Her eyes were like the little buttons on a throw pillow.

Sandy spoke up. "Oh, were you eating?"

"Why, yes. Are you doing a survey on suppers?" She laughed at her own joke.

"No," I said. "We just want to know what happened to Mr. and Mrs. Jenkins. They sent us their telescope. We came over to thank them, but they've moved."

The woman looked at us for a few moments. Her eyes changed slowly to rounder, caring eyes. "That's right. I've seen you children at Alfred and Mertle's before. Which one of you is Matthew?"

"I am."

"I'm the one who sent you the telescope, Matthew. It's supposed to be for all of you. That's what Mertle told me." She looked at our faces through the screen, and a sadness came over her. She walked out onto the porch and sat on an aluminum lawn chair that looked barely strong enough to hold her up. Some feeling, like when I lost my dog Lucas, came into my stomach, and my legs felt barely strong enough to hold themselves up.

"Mr. Jenkins passed away about two weeks ago. It was pretty sudden, though he hadn't been well lately. Mertle took it as well as could be expected, seeing how they'd been together for more than fifty years. Gracious, I think they even knew each other as children. Well, she didn't want to live here no more. Too many memories, she said. She decided to move in with her brother in Minneapolis. So she sold the place. It went fast. Old houses these days go within hours, it seems. Anyway, Mertle, she stops over here the day she's leaving and gives me five dollars to pay for the delivery of that telescope. She said she wouldn't have any kind of view from her brother's apartment. The stars and the moon would just look like another streetlight. She said to give the telescope to the kids. At night, she'd think about you using it."

I felt just like the time I got hit on the back of the head with a big rock. I was so surprised I didn't feel anything for a while. Then something inside me felt like it had broken off and was falling, falling. And there was nobody to catch it, or put it back where it belonged. It flew all around inside me for a minute. Finally the thing that had broken off found its way to the place just behind my eyes and tried to get out. I held back the tears, though. It was scary to think of letting them out. I didn't know what would happen.

The Stillwater hills seemed steeper than usual on our way home. Nobody said anything all the way back. Tommy didn't even ask any questions. I don't remember eating much for supper that night, and I went to bed early.

During the little time I slept, I had a bad dream about my dad. Dad heard me. I must have yelled in my sleep. When he came in to see what was the matter, I reached out and squeezed him around the neck until I just about choked him. "Dad, don't you or Mom ever die on me. Promise me you won't. Okay? It would be so terrible! I just had a terrible dream."

"Okay, Matthew, settle down now." I was breathing really fast and felt like I was getting dizzy. "Lie back down. I'm just fine and your mother is just fine."

"Dad, you're gonna die some day, aren't you?"

Dad smiled gently. "Someday, I suppose, but God willing, it'll be quite a while. I don't think you have to start worrying yet. I'll tell you what, son. I'll promise you this, I'll live every day I get. That's about all we can ask for."

"It doesn't seem fair," I said, turning away from him.

"Compared with what? It's like baseball. There're just so many innings. Or you could look at it like a tennis court. You get your chance to play and then you've got to get off the court and let somebody else have a chance. If the old people didn't get off the court, there wouldn't be any room for the babies to play. Do you see what I'm saying?"

"Yeah, I get it."

"But it doesn't help much, does it?"

"No."

"Well, maybe it'll help sometime." He rubbed my head and walked toward the door.

"Say, Dad?"

"Yes, Matthew?"

"Thanks for coming in. Sorry for bothering you."

"No problem. G'night."

The next day I mostly spent in my room alone. Sandy came to the door once. When Mom called me, I didn't answer. Lunch didn't interest me and neither did supper. At supper, Mom and Dad watched me and looked at each other. I could see them out of the corners of my eyes. I excused myself and went back to my room.

I was lying on my back staring at the little bumps on the ceiling when Mom came in. She sat on the end of my bed and started paging through the telescope manual. "Mr. Jenkins's death has you really upset, hasn't it?"

"I don't feel upset, Mom, like mad or anything. I just feel yucky inside, like I died a little, too. Does that sound crazy?"

"No, that doesn't seem crazy at all. A little of you probably has died. Maybe a little of the fairytale you. The part that believes, or wants to believe, that all good people live forever. Understanding living and dying is like your baby teeth falling out. The baby teeth hold up for a while, but after you grow some they just don't do the job and they fall out. Now you've got to wait for your adult teeth to come in—and that's a new understanding about living and dying. You're starting to learn that living and dying come in pairs, like shoes."

I laughed a little. "Shoes?"

"Why, yes. Everything is only good if it has an opposite."

"I don't get it, Mom."

"Let's see." She thought for a few moments. "Summer vacation. It's only special if you've gone to school for nine months. By the end of summer, it's not special because you haven't been to school lately. School makes the vacation. Get it?"

"Sort of."

She thought for a few more moments. "Think of day and night. You can't have day if there isn't night. Night makes the day special."

"It's like you *have* to have opposites, Mom?"

"Yes, pairs. Like shoes." Mom put her hand on my cheek. "Mr. Jenkins, in a way, is now in his night. But his being there makes the day brighter. His life wouldn't have been special if there wasn't a time when he wouldn't be here. The sun has set on a beautiful day."

"Boy, I never heard you talk like this, Mom. Where did you learn all this stuff?"

"You learn most everything from living, and living is mostly loving. If you love those two old people, you could think about carrying on a little of what you shared with them."

"You mean the telescope?"

"I'm sure Mertle would be pleased, and who knows, maybe Alfred would be pleased, too."

"Yeah, I s'pose you're right. They'd probably be disappointed if I didn't use it."

"Well, you think about it some."

"Okay, Mom."

Mom stood up, kissed me on the forehead and moved quietly across the room and out the door. I wasn't too crazy about the idea of disappointing people—living or not living. I remember wondering that night if people who were dead watched people who weren't. You know, checking up on living people, kind of like guardian angels.

I have a picture of a guardian angel in my bedroom. She's really tall with a chubby, pretty face. She has blond hair that shines in the dark. She's wearing a long, pale-green dress that looks like the nightgown my mom wears sometimes. The angel is smiling and watching over these two little kids who don't see her. The kids are walking barefoot over this creaky, little footbridge that has some boards missing. The littler kid is about to step into one of the holes. The other kid is holding onto his hand, and it looks like they're both going to fall through. To make things worse, there is about a two-million foot drop-off under the bridge with horrible sharp cliffs and swirling waters. There's also a big storm in the background complete with lightning and blowing trees. If kids ever needed a guardian angel, it's those two.

I wondered what the cut-off age was for guardian angels and whether I was past it. I was past Santa Claus, the Easter Bunny, and the Tooth Fairy, for sure. I figured guardian angels probably lasted longer than those other things, but maybe not until junior high. I would be starting junior high in a few weeks, and I couldn't imagine all those guardian angels needing to hang around kids who went to different classes all day long and went to dances. I pictured three hundred guardian angels floating above their kids at a Friday-night school dance. If a boy and a girl danced together would their angels dance together, too? The idea made me laugh.

Whether Alfred was watching along with my angel or not, I decided to read the owner's manual to the telescope. Fingering through it, I was glad to see there were plenty of pictures showing how to put it together and clean it. I decided to read it the best I could. I read it over and over until it made sense.

I was surprised when I heard the music for the ten o'clock TV news. Time for Cheerios! I slid off the bed and went to the kitchen for my evening bowl of Cheerios. It was something I never missed.

When I brought my empty bowl to the sink, I leaned forward and looked out the window to check the night sky. My bowl and spoon bounced and clanked into the sink. Before they stopped bouncing, I was out the back door. I ran through the cool, wet grass and it sent a shiver up my spine. When I got past overhanging branches, I climbed up on the picnic table and jumped as high as I could.

"There it is! That's it!" I shouted. Spreading in soft streaks of white were the northern lights, just like Alfred had told me. I'd never seen them before.

I lay on my back watching the sky. I watched for a long time. Mom flicked on the outside light to see what I was doing. Running to the back steps, I whispered Thank-you to Mertle and Alfred and whoever else was listening.

Chapter 16

August is the summer month I usually like least. It's the end of something fun and free, and it's very close to something not fun or free—school. In the summertime I feel just as smart as anybody and sometimes smarter. Nobody cares if you can read and this summer nobody knew I couldn't. At least I thought nobody knew.

The parts I hate about school are reading and writing stuff down. I can't do it as well as other kids my age, so it's embarrassing. Sometimes I used to get angry and felt like screaming and throwing the stupid book against the blackboard. That was before I had a lot of tests and started getting some special help with my reading and writing. I'm not asked to read aloud in class anymore, which makes me feel a whole lot happier. Once in a while, a substitute teacher comes in and calls on me to read. I just tell them I don't read. The sub watches me, figures out I'm not trying to be a wise guy, and calls on somebody else. I really would like to read like everybody else in class, but I can't yet.

There were about three weeks to go before school started. I wanted the summer to finish off big and hoped there was time for one more adventure.

The Monday morning after I saw the northern lights, I headed straight for the telescope and started putting it together. Reading the owner's manual really helped, but I also remembered pretty well how things looked. It used to be that, if I looked at things long enough, I could usually figure out how they went together. If that didn't work, I looked at the pictures. If that didn't work, I looked at it some more and started experimenting until I got it right, wrecked it, or until somebody showed up who could read the instructions. Now I found that, with lots of patience, I could read the instructions. Reading fifteen minutes a day seemed to be helping some, and I liked reading about astronomy.

Sandy and Tommy came over after breakfast and we carried the telescope out onto our sidewalk and spread the tripod. Disappointment set in because there was nothing faraway enough to look at during the day. We decided to take the telescope to the cave where the view would be better.

By flipping through the different lenses, we found the ones that were right for looking at the St. Croix River Valley. We liked watching the big cabin cruisers best. They moved out of the marina across the river from Stillwater. The boats looked like whales carrying tanned people in bathing suits that never seemed to be wet. We could just make out the pop or beer can labels.

After lunch that day Tommy, Sandy, and I heard Laura coming to join us. She was very excited. I couldn't understand anything she said as she came up the ladder because she wasn't able to talk with her hands. As she reached the cave entrance, she said, "People are stealing boats!" Laura unfolded a newspaper from her back pocket. It was an article from *The Stillwater Times*.

Sandy picked up the paper and read it to us. The headline read, "**Boat Thefts at Berger's Marina**." There was a small picture of Laura's uncle, Herb Berger. Sandy continued,

Wisconsin's St. Croix County Sheriff's Department is baffled by the theft of two boats last week. The disappearance of the boats is similar to other thefts that have occurred over a thirty-mile stretch of the river. Marinas on both the Minnesota and Wisconsin sides of the river have been raided. Both boats, stolen on different nights, were speedboats valued at approximately $15,000. The night watchman reports that he has no idea how the boats are being stolen. "I'm in or around the office most of the time so I can see where the boats are pulled out of the water. And they couldn't be towing boats out of here because I can hear any boat motors in the harbor or in the channel that goes out to the river. It's like they're disappearing into thin air."

Sandy set the paper down for a moment. "Laura, didn't your uncle tell you about this?"

She shook her head no as she breathed hard. She said that he probably didn't want her to worry. "I hate being treated like a baby. They think I'm stupid just because I'm deaf."

"You aren't stupid," Sandy, Tommy, and I told Laura.

I kept thinking about the boat thefts. "That's weird," I said, wrinkling my nose. "How are they getting those boats out of there?"

Tommy spoke up, "Maybe a UFO is coming down and stealing them."

"UFOs?" I asked. "Why would space people want speedboats. I can't picture a bunch of little green people waterskiing on the Mars canals." Tommy, Sandy, and I chuckled at the idea. Laura looked through the telescope toward the marina, directly across the river from us.

"From here," I said, "we should be able to see everything. We've got a view like no one else. We should have been here the night they stole the boats. I'll bet we would have seen the whole thing." Then I had an idea that would help Laura's uncle and get us another adventure.

"Say," I said excitedly, "why don't we camp here overnight? We could take turns looking through the telescope. From up here we should be able to see anything fishy, like lights moving around in the marina. Maybe we could find out how the boats are being stolen and tell Laura's uncle. Maybe he and Mrs. Berger wouldn't treat her like a two-year-old then."

"I don't know," Sandy said. Sandy never jumps into anything new.

Then I signed everything as best I could for Laura. Laura's face lit up when she understood what I was talking about. "Count me in," she said, her green eyes sparkling.

"I've never camped outside before," Tommy said with a worried look.

"You've never camped out before?" I asked. Tommy shook his head. "That's all the more reason. We could have a little campfire at the entrance to the cave and take two-hour shifts. One person watches while the other three sleep."

"I don't know," Sandy said, looking out at the river.

"Listen," I said, "we could take some time to watch the sky, too. Last night I saw the northern lights. Maybe they'll be out again. You wouldn't want to miss that, would you?" Sandy was weakening. Camping, solving crimes, telescopes, *and* northern lights are too much for any kid to turn down.

"Well . . . I s'pose we could try it," Sandy said.

We all decided to get permission. It wasn't easy. Parents can think of more reasons for not letting a kid do something than a kid could ever rehearse for. We did our best, though.

The four of us practiced asking permission for a good hour. One person would play the parent and say

No. Sandy was great at it. Then we'd take turns trying to convince the parent why we should be allowed. We decided not to say "Everybody else can do it" because that always backfired. We practiced sad faces and hopeful faces. We practiced describing the fort without telling our parents that it was on a cliff. Adults wouldn't understand how safe it really was. We could say it was waterproof, out of the wind, and well made. You could jump on the roof and it wouldn't even budge. At supper, we each had a chance to see if our practice would pay off.

Mom wasn't too sure about me camping with girls. I think I knew what she was getting at, but she never did come out and say. I acted like I didn't have any idea what she was talking about and she dropped it.

Laura couldn't get permission from the Bergers. She was furious and hurt. I hadn't seen her this mad before. Deaf people get mad like anybody else. Her jaw was closed tightly and her lips were squeezed together so hard that they looked white. When she signed to us that the Bergers wouldn't let her camp out, her hands moved really fast in little karate chops. She stamped her feet and paced back and forth. That girl was mad.

Sandy and Tommy came to the cave with better news. "Tommy and I got permission without too much trouble. Once they found out you would be there, Matthew, they gave right in. Besides, Mom said letting us camp in the woods behind the house seems pretty harmless after almost losing a child to a car accident."

Although Laura couldn't camp out, she stayed and helped us set up the camp that evening. We tried not to act too excited about the night ahead. Sandy and I talked about how terrible the mosquitoes would be and how it looked like it might rain and we'd probably have to go home. About eight-thirty, Laura climbed onto the ladder, looked at us and signed, "See you later."

Chapter 17

Clouds were somersaulting quietly downstream following the St. Croix waters. As night fell, they turned from white in a twilight sky to dark in a night sky.

Tommy would take the first shift watching the river. A few boats scurried back to their docks before the night fell too hard. Tommy was to wake us up if he saw anything unusual. The trouble was Tommy had never camped before, so everything was unusual to him. In addition, Tommy didn't have much luck making things out through the telescope. I decided to stay up with him through his shift.

"I think I see something," Tommy said when he first looked into the telescope. "It's big and round. It could be a UFO," he said seriously. Sandy shook her head. "It's moving!" he said in a startled voice.

"Tommy, that's the back of Sandy's head. You've got the telescope aimed too low."

"Oh," he replied. I aimed and focused the telescope at the river. Then I sat back in my lawn chair to watch the river.

We had a wonderful view of the dark new-moon sky from our cave entrance. I had never been at the cave at night before, so it seemed like a new place. A breeze seemed to come from directly above us. Looking up, I could see stars twinkling as though they could feel the breeze, too. I pretended that all the stars were little campfires and ours was just one more in a giant forest. There were more stars out than I had ever seen before. I picked one just under the Big Dipper for myself. Maybe, I thought, on our way to heaven, we stop at our own star, like at a campfire, to warm ourselves along the way.

At eleven o'clock Sandy took over, so Tommy and I crawled into our sleeping bags and quickly fell asleep. It seemed like I had only slept a few seconds when a nudge woke me. Sandy whispered something that I didn't get the first time.

"What?" I said.

"I hear something down on the path," Sandy whispered. I was too groggy to be afraid.

"It's probably just the wind. Good night." I plopped my head back down. Then Tommy's chains, which were fastened to the ladder, began to jingle. Suddenly, I wasn't sleepy anymore. Something or somebody was coming up the ladder.

"Who's there?" Sandy shouted. There was no answer, only more footsteps. I grabbed the flashlight. Just as I turned it on, Laura's head appeared at the top of the ladder.

"Hi," she said, smiling widely.

"What are you doing here? How did you ever get permission?" I asked, as I caught my breath. Neither

Sandy nor I knew the sign for "sneak out" but it wasn't too hard to figure out. Laura had talked the Bergers into letting her camp out on their screen porch. After Mr. and Mrs. Berger were asleep, she slipped out the porch door.

"I'm doing my shift!" she signed sternly. Laura was a gutsy kid.

While Tommy and I slept, Laura stayed up with Sandy for her shift. I remember the two of them talking in the dark. Laura turned her flashlight at Sandy and Sandy turned her flashlight at Laura so they could see each other as they signed.

I listened to the wind in the trees. It came in waves of sound as if the woods around us were breathing. Each breath in the trees made my eyes a little heavier and soon I slept.

At three o'clock Laura woke me. She said she didn't see anything funny at the marina. She waved good-bye as she went down the ladder and back to the Berger's porch.

My shift would last until five o'clock. It was completely quiet except for Sandy's snoring. Every couple of minutes I looked through Tommy's binocular across the river at the marina. Then if I saw anything at all, I'd hop up and look through the telescope. The rest of the time I just sat there. It was a nice time to think.

I thought about all kinds of things. I thought about my new friends. They weren't like any friends I'd had before. A slow learner who asks a lot of questions, a girl who is better at sports than me, and a gutsy red-haired girl who can't hear. I liked them. I thought about being called a hero and the parade. I thought about our cave, Mert and Al Jenkins, and the telescope. I was sure one of my new teachers would ask the class to write about summer vacation. I had enough to write a hundred pages already, and here I was in the middle of the night looking for crooks through a telescope. I told myself we were doing it for Laura's uncle. That was true, but we were doing it for ourselves, too.

The sky began to lighten. Birds started squawking and squeaking and whistling. A few cars and trucks buzzed across the Stillwater bridge. It had been a great night, even though we didn't see any crooks or northern lights.

Tommy rolled over in his sleeping bag. "What time is it?"

"It's five o'clock," I yawned. First thing in the morning Tommy asks a question.

"Did you see any robbers, Matthew?"

"No, but I saw some bats flying around. And your sister snores."

"I do not snore," Sandy said, rolling over in her sleeping bag.

"You do, too," I replied.

"No way!"

"Next time I'll bring a tape recorder. I'll prove it," I said.

"There's not going to be a next time," Sandy said, sitting up. She scratched her face.

"Yeah, there is," I answered. "We didn't see the crooks last night. We have to come back tonight."

"Not me. I've got mosquito bites on my face, my back is stiff, and there's no bathroom here." Sandy got up, threw her sleeping bag over her shoulder, and headed for the ladder. "See you and Tommy about noon. I'm going back to bed." Sandy stepped onto the ladder and disappeared.

"How about you, Tommy?" I asked. "Are you coming back tonight? Are you giving up already?"

"I have to go to the bathroom." Tommy was standing now and starting to dance around a little.

"See you later, Tommy," I said. Tommy went down the ladder without using his chains. I followed him to be sure he didn't fall going up the bigger ladder.

I walked into my house just as the sun was coming up. Mom and Dad were eating breakfast. I went into the living room to watch cartoons on TV, and fell asleep until eleven.

"Matthew," Mom said, waking me. "Laura's at the door."

"Laura?" I got up and stumbled toward the door.

Mom asked, "Didn't you get any sleep last night? You look beat. I'm not going to let you camp out anymore unless you get some sleep next time. I won't have you walking around like a zombie."

"I stayed up kind of late, but I'm okay," I said. Mom went downstairs to do some wash.

Laura sat with me while I ate my Cheerios. I told her that we didn't see anything last night after she left. Laura usually watches my mouth and my hands when I talk. She said it's easier if she can see both. She told me I didn't have to talk while I signed because she couldn't read my speech when I was chewing anyway.

I told her that Sandy wasn't going to camp anymore and I wasn't too sure Tommy would either. Laura was still so excited about watching the marina that I caught some of her excitement. We came up with a two-part plan so we wouldn't have to stay at the cave all night.

Part One of the plan was that Laura and I would just do two shifts a night for the rest of the week. Laura would do the first shift, from midnight to one o'clock, and I would do the second shift, from one o'clock to two. We guessed that's when the marina would be most quiet. Laura would sneak out of the porch where she was sleeping. She has a special alarm clock that blinks a bright light when she's supposed to wake up. I got permission to camp in my pup tent in the backyard, if I promised to get more sleep and not take five-hour naps during the day. Later, when Sandy and Tommy got up, we told them the plan. Tommy decided he would sleep in the tent, too. Sandy was out of Part One. She was through camping, but she was willing to listen to Part Two.

"Part Two goes like this," I said. "If anyone sees something fishy at the marina, he or she wakes the others. Then we get on our bikes and spy on the crooks to see how they steal the boats. The next morning we tell the Bergers how the boats are being stolen."

Sandy rolled her eyes. "Oh, sure! Okay, you can count me in. Sure. No problem." Sandy didn't sound like she meant it, but she'd said Okay, so I didn't say anything. Sandy and Laura went off together.

Tommy and I got the pup tent set up by suppertime. I brought out a windup alarm clock and set it for one o'clock. We got sleeping bags, a radio, flashlights, and bug spray. Tommy had his pocket tool kit and a roll of twenty-pound fishing line.

"What's the line for, Tommy?" I asked.

"You never know."

"I s'pose you're right, Tommy," I said. "You never know. I think we've got a good plan. Does Sandy have the bikes ready?"

"No."

"What do you mean, no?" I asked.

"She says she was only kidding. Nothing will happen anyway."

"She's not going to come to the marina?" I asked Tommy.

"No."

I thought for a minute. "Tommy, where's Sandy now?"

"She went fishing with Laura and Mr. Berger."

"Tommy," I said, "come with me and bring your fishing line! I know how we'll get her to come with us."

Monday night Laura saw nothing. I went down to the cave at one o'clock. I saw nothing. Tommy slept. Next morning, Sandy didn't want to talk about it.

On Tuesday night Laura saw nothing. I saw nothing. Tommy slept. Sandy didn't want to talk about it.

On Wednesday night, Laura saw nothing, I saw a big cabin cruiser come up the river and stop for about forty-five minutes. It was on the upriver side of the bridge with its lights out. Then it turned around and came back down the river. It didn't stop by the marina or go in, so I didn't think too much of it. I forgot to say anything about it.

The next afternoon, Laura ran over to see me. "Matthew, another boat was stolen! My uncle is mad. They don't know how it happened."

"I didn't see anything last night, did you?" I asked. Laura shook her head. "The only thing a little weird last night was that big cabin cruiser." I told Laura all about the boat, and how it parked and then left after a while.

"That's it," Laura said.

"What's it?" I asked.

"That big boat. It was there last night and a boat was stolen. Maybe it pulls the boats down the river."

"I don't know," I said. "How would it get boats out of the marina?"

Laura shrugged.

"Well, I'll go for two more nights, Laura. I'm starting to miss my bed."

"Okay," Laura answered. "If we see that big boat again, we'll ride our bikes to the marina and watch, right?"

"Yep," I answered, "that's Part Two of the plan."

"Sandy, too?" Laura asked.

"She said she would," I replied. "Since you're using Sandy's bike, Sandy can give Tommy a ride on his big three-wheel bicycle. I don't think he can drive down the hills alone. They're too steep."

On Thursday night neither of us saw the cruiser. I was getting tired of getting up in the middle of the night, and I was starting to feel foolish.

The next night—Friday—would be the last, one way or the other. Tommy decided to get up with me this time. Either Laura was going to wake Tommy and me in the pup tent or we would wake her on the porch.

Laura's last shift was quiet. When I took over the watch, she didn't have much to say except goodnight. She hung her head as she went down the ladder.

At one-twenty I looked down the river and saw something through the treetops. There were lights. "Tommy, look!" I said. We followed the lights upriver with the telescope. There was the cruiser. My heart started pounding, and the hair on my arms stood up. The boat slid under the Stillwater bridge and stopped on the other side. "Oh, oh," I said to Tommy. "Here we go. Come on, let's get Sandy and Laura." We grabbed our flashlights, and headed for the Larson's house. When we got to the house, Tommy helped me drag the picnic table over to Sandy's bedroom window.

I climbed on the table. Sandy's room was dark, but the window shade was up. I found the piece of fish line just where Tommy and I had rigged it. The end stuck out three feet through the window screen. Tommy and I had snaked the almost invisible fishing line along the wall behind Sandy's stuffed animals. The other end was tied to the corner of Sandy's blanket that was tucked in at the foot of her bed.

I yanked back hard on the fishing line. Her covers were suddenly pulled off and onto the floor. She gasped and sat up in her bed. I turned the flashlight on my face and put my finger on my lips so she'd stay quiet.

Sandy pounded her fists on the bed and stomped over to the window. "Are you crazy? What are you doing?" She was whispering and shouting at the same time.

"Shhh," I whispered. "Don't wake anybody up. We gotta go!"

"Go where?"

"Down to the marina. We saw the boat. It's there now. Come on. You and Tommy have to go on the three-wheeler."

"No way!" she said, shaking her head.

"You promised," I reminded her.

"Did not."

"Yes, you did. You said we could count you in."

"I didn't mean it." Sandy said. "You knew that."

I was frustrated. "How are we supposed to tell when you're serious or not?" I knew when I said it, it was the wrong thing to say. Sandy didn't say anything. She just turned around and picked her blanket up off the floor, climbed back into bed and covered herself.

—165—

"Tommy," I said, "I don't think she's coming."

"She didn't answer your question," Tommy said.

"I know. She's ignoring us. I hate that. Let's go ourselves. We don't need her. What do you say?"

Tommy waited a little bit before he answered. "Okay," he answered, smiling.

When I hopped off the table, I spotted the end of the fishing line shining off the light of the flashlight. "Tommy, I bet she can't ignore this." I took the end of the fishing line and gave it a good yank. "Let's go, Tommy!"

Chapter 18

Tommy and I ran lightly over the dew-spotted grass. We ran along the side of the Berger's darkened house toward the porch. Tommy tripped over a hose so hard I thought he was hurt. But he jumped right up and ran behind me to the porch door. Laura was sleeping soundly and the porch door was locked from the inside.

"Laura," Tommy whispered.

"She's deaf," I whispered to Tommy.

"I forgot," he said.

"What are we going to do?" I asked. "If we call her loudly enough so she can hear, we'll wake up the whole neighborhood."

We tried waving our hands and hissing, but Laura didn't budge. We shined the flashlight on her, but she had her back to us.

"Hey," I whispered. "We've got to get going. It's getting late. Come on."

As we ran around the corner of the house, I tripped over the garden hose and did a somersault just like Sandy had taught me.

"Stupid hose," I muttered, brushing grass off myself.

Tommy burst around the same corner, and tripped over the same hose. He fell flat on his stomach. "Dumb hose," he said in a loud voice. I hushed him. I grabbed the end of the hose to throw it to the side. Water from the hose splashed up on my face, making me blink. An idea hit me. "Tommy, wait here!" I grabbed the end of the hose and turned on the faucet on the side of the house.

"What are you going to do with that?" Tommy asked. Without answering I pressed my thumb over the end of the hose until I had a fine spray. I ran around to the front of the porch and shot the water spray through the screen toward Laura. She jumped and looked around. Tommy flashed the light on her again. When he saw that Laura couldn't see, he turned the flashlight on his face, holding the flashlight below his face and pointing it upward. The light from that angle made him look like a spook. That's what Laura saw when she turned around again. She squealed and dove back under her covers.

After a few seconds she peeked through the covers and saw it was us. Quickly, Laura hopped to her feet and was out the door.

We ran around the corner of the house to the bikes waiting for us by the garage. I tripped on the hose again! This time I didn't somersault. Instead I fell flat on my face and slid forward about five feet on the wet grass. I lay there for a few seconds deciding if anything was broken. Then I got so mad I hopped up and attacked the hose.

Next thing I knew Laura yanked me by the arm and we ran as fast as we dared to the waiting bikes. There, leaning over Tommy's three-wheel bike staring at one of the wheels, was Sandy. She stood up quickly.

Always first with the questions, Tommy asked, "Sandy, are you coming to help us catch the robbers?"

"No. I couldn't get back to sleep, so I came out to check your bike — to see if it's okay and everything."

I couldn't see Sandy's face too well in the dark, but her voice sounded different, nervous.

"And guess what," she said, "one of the back tires is flat."

"Oh, nuts!" I said. "Now what?"

"Oh, nuts!" Tommy repeated.

"And you know what else," Sandy added, "this front tire is flat, too." I bent down and squeezed the tires. Flat. Both of them. Laura reached down and squeezed the tires, too. Then she pointed to the bike pump mounted on the frame of my bike.

I had forgotten it was there. I grabbed the pump. Quickly attaching it to one of the tires, I began pumping as fast as I could. Sandy walked over to me, put her hand on my left arm, and asked, "How's it going?"

"Slowly, but I think it's holding air."

Sandy's fingernails dug into my arm. "No, Matthew," she said in a firm voice, "I think it's still leaking. Don't you?" Her fingernails dug in a little deeper. I stopped pumping. Sandy let up. I started pumping again. In went her nails. I stood up.

"Tommy," I said, "we've got a problem."

"What?"

"These tires just won't pump up. Is that the way you see it, Sandy?"

Sandy nodded and let go of my arm.

"Okay, Tommy," I said, rubbing my arm, "it's time for Plan B."

"Plan B? What's Plan B?" Sandy added.

"Let's see," I said, trying to buy time. "Humm . . . It's right on the tip of . . . Okay, that's right, yes! Plan B. You and Sandy go down to the cave and watch the river. Yep, that's it. We need you to watch the river."

Sandy had her hands on her hips. "Matthew, isn't Plan B where Tommy and I go home to bed?"

"No," I said, "that's Plan C. This is Plan B."

"What do we watch for?" Tommy asked.

"The unexpected," I said, while kicking up the stand of my bike. Laura was ready to go, riding in little circles on the driveway.

"What's 'the unexpected'?" Tommy asked.

"Um, I can't tell you," I answered, "or it wouldn't be unexpected." I pushed off and swung my leg over the seat. "Just keep your eyes open. We're counting on you guys."

Laura and I rolled down the driveway toward the street. Just as we started to turn Sandy ran up alongside me. I stopped. The streetlight shone on her and made her face glow. With her blond hair shining and her long white robe, she reminded me of the angel picture in my room—the angel who protects kids from danger on the bridge. She looked like she was going to tell me something. Instead, she just smiled and said, "Thanks." Then Sandy turned and ran off after Tommy, who was already heading through the darkness toward the cave.

Normally, a person would walk his bike down Valley View Drive. It's the hill Tommy almost went down in the car, but since we were so late, we decided to chance it. The bikes picked up speed, and we dropped to the valley below like two bombs from the sky. I kept braking all the way down the hill. I prayed that the brakes would hold. The trees sped by faster and faster. My windbreaker pulled back against my arms and chest. The loose material at the sides flapped back and forth in the wind like the wings of a blackbird.

We whooshed around the sharp curve halfway down the hill. Ahead, the streets of Stillwater waited. It didn't seem possible, but the bikes picked up more speed. The air felt cooler as we neared the bottom of the hill. Suddenly, we were at the first intersection.

"Look," Laura called out, pointing "A stop sign!" Before she got the words out, we flew past the sign. There was a car ahead of us going the same way we were. We were going so fast we had to pass him. I had one of those squeeze horns on the front of my bike, so I gave the car a little oo-gah, oo-gah as we went by.

The streets flattened as we entered Stillwater's business section, so we finally slowed down. As we rounded the corner at Briar Street, we could see the bank's clock. It was one thirty-five. Putting our heads down, we pedaled our hardest through the shadowy streets.

The only sounds were our heavy breathing and the clicking sound that Laura's bike pedal made every time it passed the kickstand. We stopped at the red traffic signal on Main Street.

Laura took her hands off the handlebars and slid the first two fingers of her right hand from her nose to the same two fingers on her left hand. That was the sign for "fun." My knees were still shaking. I couldn't believe Laura thought the whole thing was fun.

The light turned green and we were on our way again. We rolled down a deserted Main Street past the drugstore. Two more blocks and we were out onto the Stillwater bridge.

A few cars were coming the opposite way. A couple of the cars honked and somebody yelled, "Get off the bridge, you stupid so and so's." We pedaled faster. Halfway across the bridge, I looked down at the water and saw a set of running lights on a big boat. The boat was heading right under the bridge. I could hear the engines purring, but I didn't dare stop since there wasn't any place for us to pull over.

"There it is!" I said, pointing downward.

Laura waved her hand for us to get a move on, so we rose up and pedaled our fastest the rest of the way across the bridge.

Once on the Wisconsin side, we steered our bikes right and down a short hill to a small stand of trees. These ran back about the length of a football field to very near the river's edge—right next to the marina entrance. We ditched the bikes in some weeds, and made our way through the woods.

Slipping out of the trees we dropped onto our bellies so we could move through the tall grasses without being seen. We made our way to the narrow channel that joins the marina to the river. There we found ourselves on top of a five-foot wooden wall that holds back the earth on the sides of the channel. Below, the water made little splashing sounds against the wooden walls. The water looked cold, dark, and deep, so different from the blue and warm daytime waters. I felt goosebumps as I nestled deeper into the tall grasses.

We lay there for five minutes, ten minutes, fifteen minutes. Laura slid alongside me until our shoulders touched. "Where are they?" she signed.

"I don't know," I signed back. "I think they'd have to come through here. We better just keep watching."

Another five minutes passed. Still we saw nothing. I asked Laura to watch the channel while I went back upriver to see if the cruiser was still just beyond the bridge. I crawled about twenty yards through the grass. Slipping out of the weeds, I came out onto the sandy river edge. The sickening smell and remains of a dead fish were nearby. After I crawled over a little mound there was a clear view of the bridge. Its steel supports sank down into huge concrete bases that went all the way to the bottom of the river. I stared past the cement bases and into the spaces between them. The boat was parked there with its lights out. I couldn't hear the engine running, just the whirring of car tires on the bridge.

I had decided to stand up and walk back to Laura when I heard something that sounded like a big fish jumping in the water. I ducked back down again. From where I hid I could only see the tops of the little waves that caught the Stillwater lights from across the river. The waves moved steadily in wider and weaker circles until they finally blended in with the rest of the river.

I stared at the spot until I lost patience. Just as I began to stand again I heard another splash. This time, it was closer to the marina entrance. I crouched

and ran along the river in the direction of the sound. I raced by the smelly fish toward the marina entrance.

At the entrance, something again broke the water and slid back in. Whatever it was, it was big and black. I quickly found Laura.

Before I could say anything, Laura pointed to the water below us. She had seen it. "Look," she signed. Something long and black had slid into the night air from the black water. Just as quickly, it disappeared.

"What was that?" I asked, shaking my head in surprise.

Laura moved her fingers like she was tugging on the visor of a baseball cap.

"A man?" I asked. "Are you sure?"

Laura nodded and signed that he was swimming underwater.

"A scuba diver?" I said. "That's what they're doing." We settled down again to watch.

In the quiet I noticed a low sound, like scraping, coming from beneath the water. I peeked over the edge of the bank. Laura followed my cue and looked down. Then Laura tapped my shoulder. "A rope!" she signed excitedly. I stood up and grabbed Laura's arm. "Come on!" We ran as fast as we could through the darkness to find Charlie, the night watchman. Laura and I burst into the marina office, out of breath. "Charlie! They're stealing a boat!" I shouted.

"Whoa, whoa!" Charlie answered. "Who are you? And Laura, what are you doing down here in the middle of the night?"

"A big boat is stealing a little boat," Laura said excitedly. Charlie had trouble understanding Laura. She was gesturing and using short sentences. "NOW!" she exclaimed. "They're pulling the boat."

"Does your uncle know you're out running around at all hours of the night?"

Laura was getting frustrated. "They're stealing boats," she screamed, at the top of her lungs.

"Stealing boats?" Charlie asked.

"Yes," I said, "right now. There's a guy stealing one right now. We saw him."

"There ain't been anybody in here all night," Charlie said, shaking his head. "Not from the road 'cause they'd have to drive right by me, and not in from the channel neither, 'cause I can hear the boats coming in and I can see the lights, too. I keep this window open all night. It's been quiet."

"Charlie, he swam in," I said. "A guy's swimming in underwater with a rope. Then they're towing the boat out to the river."

Charlie leaned back in his chair. "Now, how would they do that?" While I was trying to explain to Charlie, Laura ran outside and down the docks toward the channel. After a few minutes I had Charlie convinced to at least take a look. Laura ran up to us just as we came out of the office.

"Look," she shouted, pointing toward the far end of the marina. I couldn't see anything. Charlie turned his powerful flashlight in that direction. Then we all saw it—a speedboat silently cutting through the black, cold water. There was no one in the boat. It was like a ghost ship moved by an invisible force.

When it disappeared into the channel, Charlie got mad. He spit and said the same word I said when I was mad at Tommy. "That boat's not going out of here tonight."

He ran off down the docks with Laura and me right behind. Charlie was a big guy, so even though he ran slowly, the floating dock sections started to bounce and bob something terrible. Laura and I had all we could do to keep from being pitched right into the water.

It was a little more than Charlie could do, though. I think he stepped onto a section of dock that was bobbing up when the section he was stepping off was bobbing down. He caught his foot, fell on his stomach, and slid right off into the water.

"Charlie!" Laura yelled. Before we had even stopped and caught our balance, Charlie popped his head up out of the water. "Ow!" he screamed. Then he spit out some water and some more words that I wasn't supposed to hear.

"Are you okay?" I asked.

"No, it's my ankle," he answered. He was thrashing his arms around and splashing a lot.

"Oh, no," I thought. "He might drown." I had turned around to look for a life preserver to throw him when Laura pushed one in my hand. She had grabbed one out of a nearby boat.

"Charlie, quick!" I called, "here's a life preserver." I was kind of nervous so I threw it pretty hard. It landed right on his head. Boy, was I surprised when he took it off his head and threw it back at me.

"I don't need this! It's only about five-feet deep here! I'm standing up."

After I signaled to Laura that Charlie wasn't drowning, the two of us followed his instruction to find a ladder. He needed help to climb back onto the dock. By the time we found the ladder, got Charlie out of the water, and helped him to the office, the cruiser was gone. Charlie immediately called the Bergers.

After Mr. and Mrs. Berger took Charlie home to put ice on his ankle, we found ourselves in the Berger's kitchen. Sandy and Tommy were there, too. They had been about to sneak back into their house when they saw Laura and me get out of Mr. Berger's truck.

"It's remarkable the way you kids figured this whole thing out," Mr. Berger said, shaking his head. "And Sandy and Tommy, you were in on this, too?"

Tommy spoke up. "Yep, we were on Plan B."

"I'll explain it to you later," Sandy said, cutting in.

Mr. Berger continued, "I'm amazed by you kids. Especially Laura. I owe you all a big thanks. I was losing customers."

Mrs. Berger added, "We're going to have a long talk about this running around town, but Herb and I underestimated you. I still don't understand how Laura . . . with her problem . . ."

Sandy butted in, "Mrs. Berger, Laura was the one who figured this thing out. She's smart, that's for sure. And she's a good teacher, too. She taught us all sign language."

"Yeah," I added, "the fingerspelling part even helps me with spelling and . . ."

Now it was Mrs. Berger's turn to butt in. "Okay, okay. I get the point. Maybe I should have given Laura a little more leeway. Anyway, thank you for helping out at the marina." Mrs. Berger gave Laura a big hug. Laura gave Sandy a thumbs-up.

"You know," I said, "I'm glad we figured out how the boats were being stolen, but I wish someone could have caught them."

"It's too bad," Mr. Berger agreed. "All we really would have needed was the license number of the boat. Then the Coast Guard could have picked them up."

Everyone was quiet for a few seconds thinking about how close we had been. Tommy broke the quiet. "I know the number."

Sandy and I snapped our heads toward Tommy. Mr. Berger said, "Tommy, what do you mean?"

"I know the boat number. I saw it in the telescope from our fort. I was following Plan B."

"Tommy," Sandy said, "you never said anything to me. You mean you know the cruiser's number?"

Tommy nodded, "I saw it when the boat drove under the bridge lights."

"He could never remember that whole number," Mrs. Berger said. "It's too long."

"Mrs. Berger," I said politely, "I think you should get a notepad and be prepared to write." Sandy looked at Mrs. Berger and nodded.

"MN358876231," Tommy said. Laura watched as Mrs. Berger wrote the numbers down.

"That sure sounds like a Minnesota boat-license number to me," Mr. Berger said, smiling.

"Mr. Berger," Sandy said, "if Tommy says he got the number off the boat, then that's the one you want."

Chapter 19

The first day of junior high came sooner than I thought possible. Most summers wear out by the end of August, so I'm almost glad to get back to school. This summer hadn't been like that. Too much had happened. Summer hadn't ended in the usual boring way. I needed about two more weeks to do nothing.

The Stillwater Times had some pictures and a write-up about the four of us. Tommy's boat numbers were right. The Coast Guard picked up three young men. It turned out that the cruiser belonged to the uncle of one of them. They told the uncle they wanted to use the boat for fishing. I guess they had been fishing, in a way. There were pictures of Tommy, Laura, Sandy, and me standing at the marina, smiling. The television people called to say they wanted to do a special story on us, but our parents said No. They said they thought all the attention might be encouraging us.

The school bus stop was right across the street from my house. I was out on the street before any of the other kids. The sun was just lifting its shiny head from behind the bluff across the river. Below, in the dark valley, patches of fog slowly lifted. They looked like ghosts rising from a graveyard on Halloween.

The tops of the trees caught the first sun of the Minnesota morning. The streetlight blinked off above me. Birds chattered, making a terrific racket. Up the street at the Berger's house, the yard light reflected off the front door as it opened. Laura stepped out, squinted my way, and waved. She walked toward me in a long furry green robe and untied tennis shoes. As she came across the wet grass, big dewdrops flew off the toes of her tennis shoes.

"I'm going home today," Laura said and signed. "Mom and Dad are coming this morning. They're back from their trip."

I could tell from her eyes that she was excited. "You'll probably be glad to see them," I said.

Laura nodded. "I will be starting school next Monday. I can't wait to see my friends."

"Well, don't forget your other friends," I said. "We'll miss you."

"You'll write to me?"

"I've got a better idea," I answered, hoping to get out of writing. "I'll call. I don't think it's long distance to Bloomington."

Laura tilted her head and wrinkled her nose at me. She tapped her ear. "I can't hear on a phone."

I had forgotten. Laura couldn't use a phone. "I'll write," I said. "Or maybe I could find one of those phones that will type you a message." I signed as I spoke.

We stood on the street for a few seconds without saying anything. I didn't really want her to go. I had had to leave all my friends in St. Paul. Now here was another friend leaving. I gave Laura a thumbs-up, then I hooked my pointing fingers together. First the right hand over the left, then the left hand over the right. She grinned and returned the sign. It meant "friend." Then Laura hugged me. She turned, waved, and walked back through the wet grass.

Tommy and Sandy stepped outside their house. They stopped on the lawn and talked to Laura for a few moments. When Tommy started to leave, Laura stopped him and gave him a big hug. Laura and Sandy were still talking as Tommy arrived at the bus stop.

"Guess what, Matthew?"

"What, Tommy?"

"Thomas."

"Why do you want me to call you Thomas?"

"It's more grown-up," Tommy stated flatly, then he continued, "A guy called last night. He wants me to be on the float next year. The one with the bear. The man said I did good. My dad said the sign should say 'Thomas.'"

"That's great! Hey, that's the float I was on."

"I know. Is it scary with all those people watching?" Thomas asked.

"Are you kidding? After what we did this summer, it'll be easy. Besides, I can show you everything about it. I'll even show you the professional parade wave."

"What's that?" Tommy wanted to know.

"It's like this." I showed Tommy. "You move your arm back and forth really slow. That's how they do it. You can wear my buckskin outfit if you want to."

"Okay."

"And I'll show you how to throw the candy so the little kids can get it but the big kids can't. Then there's a way to squint your eyes so they're almost closed, but not quite. It makes you look like you've been out on the range ropin' dogies most of your life."

Tommy tried it. "Try it without your glasses," I suggested. "Yeah, that's better. Pioneers never wore glasses."

"But I can't see," Tommy complained.

"That's okay. You don't have to see up there on the float. Just wave and throw candy. That's it."

"I want my glasses on."

"Naw, without them, when you squint, you look like an old bull. That's the look you want. Take my word for it. It's a lot better that way."

"Thomas," Sandy said walking up to us, "what are you doing?"

"I'm practicing for the parade. Matthew's going to be my coach."

"Yeah, I'm going to teach him everything he needs to know," I said, looking around at Sandy. I blinked a few times. Sandy was wearing dressy shoes instead of her blue tennis shoes. I think she had some makeup on. Her eyelids looked blue—the same color as her skirt. Her eyelashes looked darker and she was wearing tiny pearl earrings.

Sandy looked older. She looked pretty, too, but I didn't say so. I didn't feel like I was with the Sandy I knew anymore. Sandy used to punch me on the arm all the time. I was black-and-blue most of the summer. I even punched her back sometimes. I didn't think I would be able to punch her anymore. I felt more like I did when I was on the float with Miss Stillwater.

Sandy wrapped her arms around her new notebooks the way I had seen the high-school girls do in St. Paul. It made her seem older.

"Laura," she said, "thought maybe she would come back next summer. She's even going to try to visit during Christmas vacation."

"Yeah," I said standing a little straighter, "that would be fun. I promised to write to her. She can't use the phone, you know, unless it's a special typing phone."

"Yes, I know that."

"I know that, too." Tommy added.

Tommy began looking through his backpack for something. "I forgot my lunch," he said, looking nervously down the hill for the bus. "I'd better get it."

"Hurry up, Thomas," Sandy said, "if the bus comes I'll ask the driver to wait." We watched Tommy run his peculiar run to the house and disappear inside.

Sandy turned around and looked right at me. "Matthew, can I say something, something personal?"

"I guess so," I answered.

"Living with Tommy, I mean Thomas, has taught me some things. One of them is that a lot of things go into being smart. Thomas is smart in some ways I'm not. He can remember things that no one else in our family can."

"What does that have to do with me?" I asked, watching the bus groan up the steep hill.

"What I'm trying to say is this—you don't have to prove anything to me. If a hundred different things go into being smart, it doesn't mean you're not smart if you only have ninety-nine."

"Ninety-eight," I said, "I don't write too well, either."

"You know what I mean," Sandy said, grinning.

I felt better. She didn't think I was stupid. Suddenly, Sandy leaned forward and grabbed my arm. I thought she was going to punch me again so I gritted my teeth. Instead, she gave me a funny look, the kind I've seen high-school girls give boys. For a second I didn't hear the bus screech to a stop beside us. Sandy seemed different. Things weren't quite the same anymore, I knew. It made me a little sad and, at the same time, it made me happy. Then my thinking was cut short by a perfectly placed punch on my arm.

"Ouch! What's that for?" I groaned, rubbing my arm.

"I don't know. Let's get to school." Sandy smiled, quickly turned her head, and bounded up the steps onto the bus. Maybe, I thought, things hadn't changed all that much.

Up the street Tommy barreled out the front door of his house with his lunch in hand. I stood on the curb looking at the steps of the bus before me. School was about to begin again. Some of my bad feelings about school started to come back. Part of me was afraid to go up those steps.

Tommy ran up to me. "Matthew, aren't you getting on the bus?"

"Yeah, sure. You go first, Thomas."

"Okay," he answered. "Up the steps. A lot like our ladders to the cave." Tommy stomped up to the top step and turned around to me. "But no chains. Right, Matthew?"

I knew then how Tommy felt when he had to climb the ladders. I didn't know what to expect in school this year. But Tommy had been ready for the unexpected and he did fine. I decided I was ready, too. My new friends and the special summer had made me ready.